LADY CAROLINE LAMB

Also by Antonia Fraser

NON-FICTION
Mary Queen of Scots
Cromwell, Our Chief of Men
King Charles II
The Weaker Vessel: Woman's Lot in Seventeenth-century England
The Warrior Queens: Boadicea's Chariot
The Six Wives of Henry VIII
The Gunpowder Plot: Terror and Faith in 1605
Marie Antoinette: The Journey
Love and Louis XIV: The Women in the Life of the Sun King
Must You Go? My Life with Harold Pinter
My History: A Memoir of Growing Up
Perilous Question: The Drama of the Great Reform Bill 1832
The King and the Catholics: The Fight for Rights 1829
The Case of the Married Woman: Caroline Norton –
A 19th-Century Heroine Who Wanted Justice for Women

FICTION
Quiet as a Nun
Tartan Tragedy
A Splash of Red
Cool Repentance
Oxford Blood
Your Royal Hostage
The Cavalier Case
Political Death
Jemima Shore's First Case
Jemima Shore at the Sunny Grave

LADY CAROLINE LAMB

A FREE SPIRIT

ANTONIA FRASER

PEGASUS BOOKS
NEW YORK LONDON

LADY CAROLINE LAMB

Pegasus Books, Ltd.
148 West 37th Street, 13th Floor
New York, NY 10018

Copyright © 2023 by Antonia Fraser

First Pegasus Books paperback edition December 2024
First Pegasus Books cloth edition June 2023

All rights reserved. No part of this book may be reproduced in whole or in part without written permission from the publisher, except by reviewers who may quote brief excerpts in connection with a review in a newspaper, magazine, or electronic publication; nor may any part of this book be reproduced, stored in a retrieval system, or transmitted in any form or by any means electronic, mechanical, photocopying, recording, or other, without written permission from the publisher.

Paperback ISBN: 978-1-63936-786-3
Hardcover ISBN: 978-1-63936-405-3

10 9 8 7 6 5 4 3 2 1

Printed in the United States of America
Distributed by Simon & Schuster
www.pegasusbooks.com

'*How vain are the commands of a despot, and of what avail is force against the free spirit.*'

Lady Caroline Lamb, *Ada Reis*, 1823

To my friend
Salman Rushdie
A free spirit

CONTENTS

PART FOUR: THE WISH TO LIVE

NOTE ON NAMES

(with date of birth in brackets)

Caroline alone is always Lady Caroline Lamb, occasionally called *Caro*, or *Caroline William*, as the wife of William Lamb. (1785)

Caroline St Jules, later *Caro George*, is the daughter of Lady Elizabeth Foster; married to George Lamb. (1785)

Harriet alone is always the Countess of Bessborough, born Lady Henrietta (Harriet) Spencer, Caroline Lamb's mother. (1761)

Harryo is Lady Harriet Cavendish, daughter of the Duke and Duchess of Devonshire, wife of Lord Granville Leveson-Gower, later Viscount Granville. (1785)

Little G is Lady Georgiana Cavendish, daughter of the Duke and Duchess of Devonshire, married to Lord Morpeth, later Earl of Carlisle. (1783)

Hart is the Marquess of Hartington, later 6th Duke of Devonshire. (1790)

William alone is always William Lamb; it was only from June 1828, when his father died, that he was known as 2nd Viscount Melbourne – which is outside the period of this book. (1779)

Lord Melbourne is Sir Peniston Lamb, created 1st Viscount Melbourne, legal father of William Lamb. (1745)

Lady Melbourne or *Lady M.* is Elizabeth, the mother of William Lamb. (1751)

Emily is born Emily Lamb, sister of William, and marries Earl Cowper; she later marries Lord Palmerston outside the period of this book. (1787)

Fred is the Hon. Frederick Lamb, younger brother of William, son of Lord Melbourne. (1782)

George Lamb is the Hon. George Lamb, younger brother of William. (1784)

John or *John Lord Duncannon* is the brother of Caroline; he became Earl of Bessborough after the death of his father. (1781)

Frederick Ponsonby is the brother of Caroline, son of Lord Bessborough. (1783)

Willy or *William Ponsonby* is the brother of Caroline, son of Lord Bessborough. (1787)

Bulwer is Edward Bulwer-Lytton, later created 1st Lord Lytton, the son of General Bulwer and Elizabeth Lytton. (1803)

Author Notes:
I have sometimes made minor alterations in the spelling or punctuation of Lady Caroline's letters for the sake of clarity for the reader; I have not altered the sense.

I have from time to time given rough estimates of the value of particular sums in our own day, using round figures for convenience. The website of the Bank of England provides a proper detailed guide.

BREAKING THE RULES

Lady Caroline Lamb broke the rules. These were not the acknowledged rules of Church and State. Although her life was certainly not without sin, in the way the Church understood the word, it was the unacknowledged, powerful rules of Society which were broken so flamboyantly by Lady Caroline Lamb. In so doing she showed an independence and indeed a courage which few women emulated in the early nineteenth century. In this sense she was a free spirit.

During the process she outraged her contemporaries, notably the celebrated women who formed her family circle. In terms of history, it was to prove even more important that she outraged the admirers of Lord Byron, not only at the time but ever since. By his numerous biographers and other commentators she is frequently referred to as 'the infamous Lady Caroline Lamb'. She has not fared much better with the biographers of her husband, subsequently the Victorian Prime Minister Lord Melbourne, who are similarly united in their disapproval. In the presence of these two great men, Lady Caroline has too often been denied a balanced estimate. Just as her literary works, including three novels, have been too often considered purely for the clues they give to her personal life.

This book can be seen as a coda to my three books on early-nineteenth-century reform, the third of which concerned Caroline

Sheridan Norton, the possible mistress of Lord Melbourne, and reform of the rights of married women.

It can also be regarded as the culmination of an exciting and fulfilling life spent studying History.

Here I have attempted to write about a human being – and a woman, and incidentally a mother – who at a time of woman's submission, both legally and socially, went her own way.

PART ONE

═══════════════

EVERY WISH
OF HER HEART

*'Early loved and early won by a young man who was at
the same time a nobleman and a statesman, every wish of
her heart, every aspiration of her mind, would appear to
have been gratified by success.'*

Lady Morgan's Memoirs

CHAPTER ONE

Lovely and Lively

'A lovely little Girl – who seems very lively and in perfect health'

Countess Spencer, 1785

CAROLINE PONSONBY – THE future Lady Caroline Lamb – was born on 13 November 1785, into an exotic world. Her mother Harriet was the sister of Georgiana Duchess of Devonshire, the star of Whig Society; it was this famous aunt who would salute Caroline:

> Fairy, sprite, whatever thou art
> Magic genius waits on thee
> And thou claimst each willing heart
> Whilst thy airy form we see.

The Duchess duly gave her niece a pencil to record her own poems.[1]

Rather more soberly, Caroline's grandmother Countess Spencer, who was present, described the birth in her diary. Harriet was established in the house of her parents-in-law, the Earl and Countess of Bessborough, a handsome Georgian building at 17 Cavendish Square. It was evidently quite a long labour, although it had a happy ending. Lady Spencer was sent for at eight in the morning, to find that Harriet had been 'grumbling' since the early hours. Labour finally ended at half past four the next morning when Harriet 'was brought to bed with a lovely little Girl – who seems very lively and in perfect health'. Even if Harriet herself was 'a little low'.[2]

Caroline's petite size was emphasised from the first; she was the 'little girl' of the family following two boys, John the heir, and Frederick Ponsonby, with a further brother William born two years later. But she was also an elfin creature – a sprite in the words of the Duchess – compared to the cousins with whom she was brought up. Georgiana Cavendish (Little G), daughter of the Duchess, was born in 1783; the Duchess of Devonshire gave birth to another daughter Harriet Cavendish, always known as Harryo, a few months before Caroline was born. No one ever compared Little G or Harryo to a sprite. When the Duchess finally managed to give birth to an heir, the Marquess of Hartington, to be known as Hart, he grew up dazzled by his little fairy-like cousin, despite the fact that he was four years younger.

The closeness of the two families, Devonshire and Bessborough, Cavendish and Ponsonby, was symbolised by the fact that Little G and Frederick Ponsonby shared a christening. Not only were their respective mothers sisters, but their fathers were actually first cousins. There were however other members of the family circle equally close, yet without conventional status: there was the mysterious list of children of dubious parentage – constantly added to over the years – whose existence must surely have been baffling to the young until they were old enough to understand the truth. The contemporary phrase for them was 'Children of the Mist'. This convoluted circle of parents and children, with marriage the outsider, bore out the lament of a pamphlet published in 1785, the year of Caroline's birth: 'It is a melancholy reflection that infidelities are much more frequent among people of elevated rank than those of less exalted status.'[3]

Above all there was the seductive presence of Lady Elizabeth Foster, mistress of the Duke of Devonshire. A contemporary of the Spencer sisters, Georgiana and Harriet, Bess, as she was known, was the daughter of the Earl of Bristol, and had two sons by her husband John Foster. Her powers to charm were legendary: 'no man could withstand her' wrote one man who observed her when she was young (although hardly surprisingly the Devonshire daughters Little G and Harryo detested her). Physically Bess has been described as the opposite of Georgiana, tiny to Georgiana's magnificently glamorous appearance.[4]

Caroline St Jules, so called, was Bess's illegitimate daughter by the Duke; the elderly Comte de St Jules agreed to accept paternity. There would be a son, William Clifford, born in 1788. Caroline St Jules was actually born on 16 August 1785, four days before the Duchess gave birth to her own Harryo, implacably demonstrating that the Duke had had sex with his wife and mistress within days. As the children grew up, the extreme closeness of Georgiana Duchess and Lady Bess must have added to the confusion; the tone of their correspondence ('my dearest, dearest, Bess, my lovely friend' etc.) might almost suggest that the two women were genuine lovers. However Georgiana Duchess was not without her own, more conventional admirers. In turn she would dive abroad a few years later to give birth to Eliza Courtney, daughter of her lover, Charles Grey.

This was a grand private society with its own nicknames. Hence the Duke of Devonshire was Canis, the Duchess The Rat, Lady Elizabeth Foster The Raccoon, and so on. With merriment went notorious unpunctuality: at Chatsworth it was said that dinner was served at 4.30 p.m. but the ladies went up to dress at 5.45! Nor did religion play a great part in their lives. Fanaticism, as perceived by the Whigs, did not meet with favour: Harriet Bessborough, for example, did not approve of nuns. Theirs was not a religion of certainty. Richard Payne Knight summed it up in his poem *The Progress of Civil Society* of 1796:

Religion's lights, when loose and undefined
Expand the heart, and elevate the mind . . .
But, in dogmatic definitions bound,
They only serve to puzzle and confound . . .

Caroline herself put it more simply: alas, she did not know how to 'believe or doubt'.[5]

The upbringing of the Ponsonby and Cavendish children, privileged in many ways, deprived in others, was conducted in a variety of dwellings, from palaces to gracious houses. In the upper rooms, attended by a warren of domestics, the children flourished with frequent forays downstairs to their parents' lavish apartments. Foremost among these residences was the magnificent Palladian house in St James's, overlooking Green Park, built by Caroline's grandparents. Spencer House is described by one authority as 'the queen of London houses'.[6] Then there were the residences of her aunt and uncle: Devonshire House, also overlooking Green Park from the other side of Piccadilly, between Berkeley Street and Stratton Street, and Chatsworth, set in the countryside of Derbyshire.*

There was also a neo-classical villa at Roehampton, on the outskirts of London, conveniently near Richmond Park, which had been designed for Lord Bessborough in 1760; it was celebrated in verse:

> We seem to breathe & tread on Classic Ground . . .
> Ask ye, from whence these various Treasures came
> These scenes of wonder? Need I Bessborough name?

And in contrast there were the trips abroad – for reasons of health, a term which covered a variety of experiences, some murkier than others. As will become apparent, a great deal of Caroline's youth was spent abroad.

In 1785, the year of Caroline's birth, King George III had been on the throne since 1760, and the period of his public 'madness' had not yet commenced. The unmarried Prince of Wales – the future Prince Regent, subsequently George IV – contracted a secret illegal marriage to the Catholic Mrs Fitzherbert in December. The American Revolution had been accomplished and Independence secured; the storming of the

---

* Devonshire House no longer exists; Spencer House however flourishes.

Bastille, which marked the beginning of the French Revolution, was a few years ahead. William Pitt the Younger headed a Tory government. Whigs and Tories were not organised political parties in the modern sense and the designation was not always clear-cut; words like Conservative and Liberal were not yet in use. Politics – of a sort – permeated the lives of the Whig aristocracy into which Caroline was born: a bright young man was very likely to try for Parliament, in an age before reform of the House of Commons (Pitt for example failed to abolish so-called 'rotten boroughs') when family influence would secure a seat. A bright young woman on the other hand would expect to marry well, meaning material prosperity as well as social position.

Reform, whether successfully achieved or not, was the buzzword of the time, which the children picked up. A characteristically roguish letter from Caroline when she was twelve years old to her cousin Little G Cavendish, another infant Whig, began: 'A reform a reform, did you write a reform? then goodby cousin . . . I disdain to reform at this time. I will reform in heart but not in hand. I will reform myself but not my letters, *you lilly-livered girl.*' She then gives a glimpse of her family life: 'there is papa, mama, my brothers and I, and I am always going out in Town and then when I come here we play at battlecock and shuttledore [a children's game originating in India] and mama reads Shakespeare in the evening'. When her mother goes up to bed, Caroline continues to 'rail out a song' with her brothers in the great hall while 'the Men drink in the dining-room, them men generally are poor, Papa and some dogs lying by the fire, we go out a great deal here'. Lots of jokes on the concept of Reform followed in her letters to Little G. 'Sweet G, we will reform but not till we meet,' she wrote.[7]

In this nest of cousins, connections and friends, Caroline from the first stood out for her charm – and her wilfulness.

When her grandmother Lady Spencer described her from time to time as 'lively', she was alluding to a certain tempestuous quality, adorable or annoying in a tiny child, but apparent in

Caroline from an early stage. When she was eleven, Caroline had the wit to write to Little G:

I'm mad
That's bad
I'm sad
That's bad
I'm bad
That's mad[8]

It was a wry self-knowledge which would only develop with the years.

Caroline's father was the twenty-seven-year-old Frederick Ponsonby, future 3rd Earl of Bessborough. At the time of her birth he was known as Lord Duncannon, a courtesy title given to the heir to the earldom; he inherited the Bessborough title seven years later, and at this point little Caroline, as an earl's daughter, became Lady Caroline and John, his eldest son, Lord Duncannon.

Possessed of Irish estates in which he was thought to take little interest, as an Anglo-Irish peer Bessborough would nevertheless feel sufficiently strongly to speak out against the proposed Act of Union of 1801. A Parliamentary report of the time described him as 'a man of the most amiable and mild manners; without at all affecting the character of an orator, he is an excellent speaker'. At one point he became First Lord of the Admiralty. Bessborough was not however particularly rich nor particularly amusing, and as such he received very little attention compared to his wife, Harriet. It was significant that this Lord's amiable manners did not prevent him from shouting at her in public: on one occasion he upbraided Harriet at a party for wearing her diamonds against his wishes – which did at least attract public notice. But perhaps that was the point.[9]

His wife, born Henrietta Spencer, daughter of the 1st Earl Spencer, came from a family with a tradition of strong women: epitomised perhaps by their ancestress Sarah, the great Duchess of Marlborough, favourite of Queen Anne. Harriet suffered in childhood from being the sister of the beautiful Georgiana, although at the same time the two girls were devoted to each other. Never-theless Harriet, as she was always called, was generally dismissed as being 'an ugly little girl', except for an abundance of brown hair.[10] The effect of this dismissal on Harriet, far from subduing her, was to make her, in the absence of physical beauty, cultivate an extraordinary power to attract. A portrait of her in 1793 by Angelica Kauffman shows a young woman of distinct allure, with a sultry mouth and beckoning eyes. As she grew older, age did not seem to diminish her attraction as she developed into a commanding presence.

Married at the age of nineteen, giving birth to her eldest son the next year, it was not long before Harriet enacted that notori-ous pronouncement of Lord Egremont on the Whig world: 'There was hardly a young married lady of fashion who did not think it a stain upon her reputation, if she was not known as having cuckolded her husband.' He added: 'The only doubt was who was to assist her in the operation.'[11]

Harriet Bessborough was, as it were, assisted in the operation for a period of years by Richard Brinsley Sheridan, playwright and politician, in equal parts dissolute and fascinating. There were others including Charles Wyndham, a younger son of the Earl of Egremont, a member of the Prince of Wales's dissolute circle: many years later a famous man would dismiss Lady Bessborough contemptuously as 'the hack whore of the last half century'.[12] But the significant relationship of the years sur-rounding Caroline's birth, inevitably casting doubt on her actual parentage, was with Sheridan. The possibility that the future Lady Caroline Lamb shared the mesmerising Irish blood of the Sheridans certainly existed.*

More important to Caroline's character and upbringing than this notional genetic inheritance is the fact that she adored her fascinating, dominating mother. The sexual morals that she

* It is possible to discern a resemblance between Caroline and Sheridan's legitimate son Tom Sheridan, who would have been her half-brother. But there can be no absolute certainty either way in an age without efficient contraception.

must have observed in her dearest relation, whether they were to be emulated or rejected, could not be ignored. The chatter of innumerable servants – that unstoppable source of intimate news – meant that Caroline would inevitably have known much about her mother's so-called private life, without necessarily understanding it at the time.

The Bessboroughs however were not always quite as outwardly serene in the conduct of their private lives as the Devonshires. The Sheridan affair was not actually allowed by the future Lord Bessborough to remain in discreet Whig obscurity. Relations between the couple were bad enough for Caroline's father to institute a rare proceedings in the ecclesiastical court (the only method of divorce then legal). It was his brother-in-law the Duke who persuaded him to drop the case and leave things as they were.[13]

Gradually the tactics of the exhibitionist Sheridan began to grate on Harriet: for example he appeared in a box at the theatre and pretended to cry when she ignored him. Nevertheless, willingly or not, Harriet Bessborough remained in touch with Sheridan to the sad end of his drunken, indebted life, and even gave him money when he was in acute distress. Sheridan certainly retained something of the wayward and amusing spirit which had captivated London: found drunk in the gutter by the nightwatchman, he gave his name as the noted philanthropist and emancipator of slaves, William Wilberforce.[14] But where romance was concerned, Harriet, as we shall see, moved on.

The other strong female character in Caroline's childhood was her maternal grandmother Countess Spencer, with whom she spent a considerable amount of time, especially during her mother's journeys abroad, as in March 1790 when Harriet was in Brussels. Here the example was very different. Lady Spencer, born Margaret Georgiana Poyntz, the daughter of a diplomat, had been widowed before she was forty – two years before Caroline's birth – and thus had plenty of time to devote to her grandchildren, whom she treated with kindness and general tolerance.

Lady Spencer once told Harriet: 'The happiness of my children, I think I do not deceive myself by saying, is that on which mine entirely depends.' This meant that in order to preserve this happiness, from time to time Lady Spencer was moved to deplore any possible weaknesses in her daughters' lives. There was Harriet's 'inclination to play', for example. On one occasion, Lady Spencer advised her against going to the Prince of Wales's Ball: 'keep your heart free from the life of dissipation you seem to be plunged into' – not advice, as has been seen, that Harriet took. Unfortunately her pious hope, expressed in 1792, 'before I die, of seeing you and your sister leading useful, exemplary and blameless lives, and enjoying the calm of solid happiness that can be preserved by no other means' was not fulfilled either.[15] No doubt Lady Spencer intended to do better with the next generation.

Lady Spencer was a clever woman; widely read, she enjoyed the classics – she could read Greek, most unusually for a woman of her class and generation – as well as French and Italian. She liked playing chess. She was also genuinely pious, a keen reader of the Bible, and translated this piety into practical compassion for the poor. Lady Spencer lived at Holywell House, St Albans, where in her own words: 'Method is my hobby horse.' Lady Spencer had her weakness: the family curse of gambling which would enmesh both her daughters. But on the other hand, her philanthropic nature, combined with her intelligence, meant that she took an interest in education generally, her local village school and Sunday schools in particular.[16] This example, given to the youthful Caroline, was of a very different nature from that of her own mother.

The little girl was a good learner and could read when she was four and a half. At the age of five she even spoke some French and Italian; soon she was able to write a short letter in French. Caroline also enjoyed learning to play the harpsichord: a lifelong love of music was inculcated. A more unusual accomplishment of a very different nature was acquiring the characteristic drawl of the Devonshire House set, at once light-hearted and infantile. This drawl, originally spoken by the Cavendish family, was adopted by Georgiana Duchess. Thus China was 'Chaney', chemist was 'chimet', yellow became 'yaller', cucumber 'cowcumber' and, most characteristically, 'you' became a babyish 'oo'. Caroline wrote to her cousin Little G in a typical effusion apologising for the lack of a letter: 'oo know, dearest 'ove that I 'ave so 'ittle time for 'ose things 'at it is impossible to 'ite' – before ending more sensibly: 'Now, G, I will write to you.'[17]

These frolics, whatever impression they gave to outsiders, did not stop Caroline from being intelligent. This intelligence and enjoyment of studying and reading was combined with another passion which was to be lifelong – for dogs. Tango, Patsam, Bambina, Venture, Prince, Vixon (*sic*), Ceazer, Suvent and Jock (a roll call of her dogs at Roehampton) all played their part. On one occasion abroad, she adopted a fox cub. Later she would take in strays, as a line in her poem 'To a Lanky Cur I lov'd at that time' expressed:

> Your boasted power is over
> To the greenwood I'll repair
> There unbind my yellow hair . . .
> Breathing freely my native air
> Come follow me – Dog Rover.[18]

Dogs, she declared, were really human; the need for affection, the need to express affection, both strong emotions with Caroline, were admirably catered for by the love of dogs. Later a passion for horses and riding – above all when she could ride freely, without restrictions – joined the passion for dogs. (Caroline however refused to ride side-saddle, as ladies were supposed to do.)

Less happy, expressing another side of Caroline's developing character, was her relationship with one of her cousins, Louisa Poyntz, as reported by Lady Spencer. While Caroline was 'grown very fond of her grandmother', sleeping in her room, the independent child resisted Louisa's attempts to pet her and take her on to her lap, although Louisa 'doted on her', in her grandmother's words. Choice was already important to her. There was a deeply affectionate character developing but also a defiant little girl who would write when she was eleven: 'I have been studying . . . but Have not been able to attain the perfection of giving all the House a Headache.'[19]

Then there were her brothers, evidently rumbustious before they were despatched to public school – in their case, Harrow. This was certainly not a purely feminine world. There is a letter from Caroline to her cousin Little G of September 1797 when she was eleven: 'my brothers went yesterday to Harrow. Before they went they hunted some rats and John threw me a dead one which blooded me.' Fortunately the letter passes on to higher things: last night she had peered 'at Jupiter the star through the telescope . . .'.[20]

What did she look like, this lovely and lively little girl? Her hair was cut short, a little trimmed every day, so as to thicken it according to contemporary standards of beauty. The effect was to increase the attractive boyish style which was and would remain such a notable feature of her appearance. Her eyes were enormous in her tiny cat-like face with its pointed chin: here was, to outward eyes, something of a boy-girl, and a very attractive one whichever sex she represented.

A major disruption of this childhood, privileged in material terms at least, occurred when trips abroad began, often the product of Lady Bessborough's ill health. In the summer of 1791, at the age of only thirty, Harriet had a stroke and was seriously ill; henceforth her health would become a strong factor in deciding the course of Caroline's childhood. Altogether little Caroline would be abroad for over three years. Caroline went with both her parents to Nice in the South of France for Harriet to recover. The sons remained in England: the eldest, ten-year-old John William, would give cheerful news from Harrow: 'Dear Mama, I hope you continue to get better. Fred is very well and likes Harrow very well . . . I have got a great many lead soldiers here which we draw up in rank and file, & we have many a pleasant battle.' Although the letter did contain the more plaintive enquiry: 'Pray send me word where you are.' Fred, aged eight, struck the same note: 'I like school very much. John and I are very well, when will you come back?'[21] Her father returned to England in June

1792, but Caroline, now six,* remained with her mother to go and bathe in the healing waters of a spa. Meanwhile Georgiana's enforced expedition abroad to give birth to her daughter Eliza by her lover Charles Grey (subsequently handed over to Grey's parents) meant that she now became part of the little roving party.

Some of their encounters involved characters who would prove to be part of history, giving a dramatic flavour to their travels. In August the party visited Lausanne and had a sight of the young French princes, exiled by the fearful events occurring in France: Louis XVI, currently imprisoned, would be executed in January 1793. These were the sons of the Comte d'Artois, the Ducs d'Angoulême and de Berry on their way to join the Royalist army. The Duc de Berry was only thirteen, but according to Harriet's letter to her son John: 'The day he was 12 he wrote to his father begging him to let them come to him & fight by his side.' The little Duc had read in the Roman history that when Hannibal was twelve he took an oath to defend and revenge his father, and he was taking the same oath.[22]

But most of 1793 was spent in Italy: it was at this point that Caroline's father succeeded to the Bessborough title. William Ponsonby, the youngest boy, arrived with his father in September to join the family in Naples. There was also a meeting with Queen Maria Carolina – whose unfortunate sister Marie Antoinette, Queen of France would die beneath the guillotine in October.

One encounter however did reveal something of Caroline's mettle – her outspokenness and her eccentricity, or, as the Duchess of Devonshire put it rather more crudely, she was very naughty and said whatever came into her head. In 1792 there was a visit to Edward Gibbon at his house overlooking Lake Geneva. The distinguished historian, author of the mighty many-volumed *The Decline and Fall of the Roman Empire*, was then in his fifties, already swollen with the disease which would finally

* Caroline's mid-November birthday has the awkward effect for a biographer that for the greater part of the year she is actually a year younger than the age indicated by the calendar.

kill him. The Duchess of Devonshire described the scene to her daughter: 'Mr. Gibbon is very clever but remarkably ugly . . .'. Caroline in fact told him that his big face frightened the little puppy with whom he was playing. She did better in a sense on another occasion, as reported by Georgiana Duchess: 'One day Caroline Ponsonby out of kindness, wanted one of the footmen who had been jumping her [i.e. jumping her up and down] to jump Mr. Gibbon, which was rather difficult as he is one of the biggest men you ever saw . . .'.[23]

Caroline was ill in Italy in 1793, an unpleasant gastric attack involving worms which left her inordinately thin. But more traumatic for the future life of the child Caroline was an event which took place in Naples late in the year. Her mother fell violently in love with a young man of twenty-one, Lord Granville Leveson-Gower, son of the Marquess of Stafford, with a career in diplomacy ahead. It was a relationship which would last for seventeen years before ending in a fashion which would have seemed improbable at the start: it certainly branded Caroline's childhood. Granville was handsome and he was clever and he was amusing; furthermore he was known already to have a taste for older women. Since this was the Whig world, no particular attempt was made to cover up their relationship, merely to act elegantly as though it did not exist. But there were consequences.

Caroline's mother, Lady Bessborough, would, as a result of her affair, give birth more or less clandestinely to two children of whom Granville was the father. Harriette Stewart and George Stewart were born in 1800 and 1804.*

The story given out for the birth of little Harriette was that Lady Bessborough had had a fall in London; at which point her sister the Duchess, who was in Bognor, rushed to her rescue.[24] Whether or not there was a real fall, there was a real baby who was discreetly taken away to a foster mother. But this was an age

---

* Thus three women, the Duchess of Devonshire, Lady Bessborough and Lady Elizabeth Foster, had between them given birth to fourteen children, of whom five – over a third – were in fact bastards: all connected by cousinage or actual parentage.

of immense physical intimacy among women, in which it would have been quite impossible for the inevitable changes brought about by pregnancy to be ignored. Even though it was the custom for such babies to be given to other homes, the circumstances surrounding their actual births could not pass unnoticed.

Once again the psychological effect of such happenings on a sensitive child like Caroline can only be surmised. Above all, the influence it had on her own notion of morality must be questioned: as she gradually came to understand such developments, was she perhaps gradually encouraged by her strange circumstances to make her own rules?

For the moment however Harriet, Lady Bessborough and her daughter returned to England. Tempestuousness – that liveliness commented on by her grandmother – continued to mark the childhood of the lovely little girl. One of the governesses with whom Caroline came in frequent contact was Selina Trimmer, a pious, even puritanical woman who was part of the Devonshire household, despite disapproving of Georgiana's dissipated tastes including her gambling. Caroline saluted 'Selly' in verse:

> The Orange and the Lemon pale
> With Selly's cheek may vie:
> But ah! no maid that is not frail
> Has such a jet black eye

Much later Hart, the only son of the house, would reflect with the wisdom of hindsight: 'To teach us was enough for mortal patience', but when the wildness of Caroline was added he supposed that it was the charm which accompanied that wildness which enabled 'Selly' to put up with her.[25]

Caroline was now considered to be in need of the further discipline of an actual school. There had been incidents with other governesses, and on occasion, to calm her, laudanum was used, disguised in lavender drops. It has to be borne in mind that, rightly or wrongly, laudanum was in fact considered a useful, not an exceptional remedy at the time. In the words of one authority: 'Everybody kept laudanum in the house and used it on occasion for minor ailments and aches.' Nelson, for example, used it for pain. Caroline even wrote a poem to laudanum, containing the line: 'Lull with thy poppy wreath my soul . . .'*26

Caroline was entered into a London day school at 22 Hans Place. The school was owned by the émigré Dominique de Saint-Quentin, a French teacher, author of a French grammar, married to an English woman; it would subsequently be run by the noted educator Frances Rowden and has been described as 'an inspirational school' of above-average merit. Caroline, who had been lucky to spend time with a grandmother interested in intellectual matters, was lucky again even though her stay there did not last very long. At the end of her education, Caroline could now write poems in French and copy Italian songs into gift-books (even if she had a forgivable childish inclination to muddle the two languages). She also learnt Latin and Greek, to the extent that she read the New Testament in Greek and translated Ovid from Latin.[27]

Caroline's tastes in reading covered not only the classics, but also poets such as Alexander Pope. She enjoyed the novelists of the day including Maria Edgeworth and her future friend Sydney Morgan. She had the natural curiosity of a clever teenager: as when she wrote to her cousin Little G about the newly founded *Edinburgh Review* edited by Francis Jeffrey, 'Have you ever seen the Edinborough [sic] Review. I hear it is very good – on many new plays and books.'

December 1802 found the family back in Paris, Lady Bessborough having given birth to Harriette Stewart. In March of this year the Treaty of Amiens had been signed, bringing peace between Britain and France: a country led since 1799 by its so-called First Consul, Napoleon Bonaparte (who in 1804 would rise higher still as Emperor of the French). This was a new regime and the Whigs were eager visitors to this post-revolutionary Paris. They were in genial sympathy with political developments: Lord and Lady Holland were friends and admirers of Napoleon.

---

* A comparison might be made to the way paracetamol is regarded in modern times.

Lady Bessborough however, while sympathetic enough personally to visit France, allowed her previous friendship with Marie
Antoinette and her sister Maria Carolina to prevent her being
introduced to Napoleon.

Nevertheless she wrote to her friend Lady Melbourne of her
determination to go to evening parties for the sake of Caroline.
'Paris is going to be very gay; hitherto it has been like a new
world' where she did not recognise the faces.[28]

The family party consisted of Lord and Lady Bessborough,
Caroline and John, now termed Lord Duncannon. Young Caroline, aged just seventeen, actually made her debut at a ball in
Paris given by the Duchess of Gordon. It was something she
herself saluted – as throughout her life she greeted every major
event – in verse:

> Farewell to England and farewell to frocks.
> Now France I hail thee with a sweeping train.
> Subdued I'll bend my stubborn locks
> And enter on a life of pain
>
> Farewell to childhood and perhaps to peace
> Now life I sail upon thy dangerous stream[29]

Lady Spencer had ordered her daughter to prepare Caroline
for her official entry into the world: she should get 'one of the
best dancing masters or mistresses if there are such to teach
her how to go out and come into a room with propriety and
without embarrassment'.*[30] She also met such female luminaries
as the witty hostess Madame de Staël, and the reclining hostess
Madame Récamier; the latter inculcated in the youthful Caroline
a sympathetic desire to fling herself on sofas and relax on them.

The Caroline who returned to London – a ghastly journey for
all concerned, the worst inn ever, the bed up a ladder and shared

---

* With hindsight it is possible to say that the dancing master (or mistress)
did better at training Caroline to enter a room without embarrassment
than with propriety.

with chickens – was ready to face the more gracious world for which she had been prepared. And it would soon be time to think of marriage. There was no other respectable outcome for the life of a pretty young woman than the profession of marriage, as advantageous as possible; about the only profession open to the plain ones was some form of teaching. Ladies could earn money writing of course (and many did), but that combined happily as it has always done with marriage.

The first to go was Little G. In March 1801 she was transformed into Georgiana Morpeth when, at the age of not quite eighteen, she married Lord Morpeth, heir to the Earl of Carlisle. George Morpeth was already a Whig MP; his portrait by Thomas Lawrence showed a pleasant enough man; and a year later the new Lady Morpeth gave birth to a son also called George. It remained to be seen whether cousin Caroline and sister Harryo would do as well.

Naturally, in this gracious Whig much-intermarried world, there were candidates within the family circle. John Lord Althorp, for example, son of Harriet's brother Earl Spencer, thus Caroline's first cousin, three years her senior, was an obvious choice. He was later described by his grandmother as caring for 'neither Father, Mother, brothers, sister or for anything on earth but that noble animal, a horse'. This excessive equine passion was no disadvantage in a young man of suitably aristocratic birth, heir to a large and extremely agreeable estate in Northamptonshire.

But there was a complication. Caroline was in love.

CHAPTER TWO

Mortal Bride

*'Thus spoke Titania when she sigh'd
Doomed to become a mortal bride'*

Lady Caroline Lamb, 23 June 1805

CAROLINE WOULD RECOUNT how she had fallen in love with young William Lamb, son of Viscount Melbourne, at a party at their house. She was in her early teens and he was six years older. He was reading poetry aloud. A portrait of William about this time by John Hoppner shows a handsome young man with dark eyes beneath heavy brows, a fine aquiline nose and thick dark hair. Intensely romantic, the young Caroline was also a great lover of poetry. It is easy to believe that the combination of a good-looking young man and the book in his hand was irresistible. In fact her mother confirmed this early passion in a letter to her own lover Granville Leveson-Gower of May 1805 when the match was a *fait accompli*: 'she has preferr'd him since childhood, and now is so much in love with him that before his speaking [i.e. proposing], I dreaded it affecting her health . . .'.[1]

Caroline's confidante of later years, the novelist Sydney Morgan, referred to her as 'early loved and early won' by a young man 'who was at the same time a nobleman and a statesman'.

But this was in retrospect. At the time when the young people fell in love, the situation was not so simple.

Given Caroline's volatile nature, experienced by the families around her since childhood, her fits of fun, her fits of rage, there was some doubt – expressed for example by her mother – as to whether placid William could manage her. Duchess Georgiana on the other hand feared for the consequences if Caroline was checked, since her passionate love for William was so apparent.[2]

On the other side, Lady Melbourne questioned Caroline's 'lack of decorum', which was ironic since Caroline herself would come to question the louche manners of Lady Melbourne's own family circle:

> Yes, I adore thee William Lamb
> But I hate to hear thee say God d—[3]

Then there was the questionable status of the Lamb family. The Lambs were comparative newcomers to the aristocracy. William's father was the 1st Lord Melbourne, his Irish peerage being created in 1770, transformed first into a viscountcy, and later an English peerage which enabled him to sit in the House of Lords. Elizabeth Melbourne was born Milbanke, the daughter of a minor baronet. Furthermore William was actually a second son, who traditionally inherited little in the way of fortune and made his own way in the world. So Caroline's first love was dictated by passion, not a desire for future material gain. In the same way William's declaration, 'of all the Devonshire girls, she is the one for me', supposedly said after seeing Caroline at a party, was a romantic not a practical assertion.[4]

There was a further aspect to William's parentage, widely known in Society. Lady Melbourne, a woman both intelligent and voluptuous who was prepared to share her charms, allowed it to be known that William was actually the son of the Earl of Egremont. So, probably, were his siblings, Frederick and Emily. George Lamb, born in 1784, was deemed to be the son of a royal lover, the Prince of Wales, who was his godfather – hence his name.

Emily Lamb, eighteen months younger than Caroline, was already a figure in her life; Caroline had encountered her, together with her cousins Little G and Harryo, in childhood days at Devonshire House. Emily was infinitely beguiling: 'a little thing all eyes' in one description and 'always like a pale rose' in William's own words later.[5] She was also a deceptively strong character, with something of her mother's brilliance; time would show that she was devoted to her brother's interests. But it was of course the eldest brother Peniston Lamb, acknowledged (by Lady Melbourne) as the son of his legal father, who was in time due to inherit the Melbourne title.

Then everything changed. Peniston Lamb died unmarried, of consumption, in January 1805. William Lamb was now the heir – not only to the title but to Melbourne Hall in Derbyshire, Brocket Hall in Hertfordshire and Melbourne House in London. The Bessboroughs began to look more favourably on a match to which in any case their wilful daughter was in her own mind pledged. Harriet confided to Granville further that William's letter of proposal was beautiful, alluding to his change of circumstances: 'amongst other things,' he tells her, 'I have loved you for four years, lov'd you deeply, dearly, faithfully – so faithfully that my love has withstood my firm determination to conquer it when honour forbade me my declaring myself'.[6]

After all this romance, there was a comical scene when Lady Bessborough was able to inform William that, following his letter, Caroline had accepted his offer of marriage. They were actually behind a box at the Drury Lane Theatre. William promptly flung his arms round his future mother-in-law and kissed her. At this very moment the politician George Canning appeared and was first amazed then shocked. One can easily imagine what conclusions he drew from the sight of the notoriously fascinating Harriet in the arms of a personable young man. When he was told the rather less shocking truth of her daughter's engagement, Canning's reaction was so generous that Harriet now decided to give him a properly grateful kiss as a reward.

There was however one sad postscript to the announcement of the marriage. Hart, as the Marquess of Hartington, only son of the Devonshires, was known, had nourished through childhood a passion for his cousin Caroline, whose famous liveliness was such a feature of his upbringing; despite the fact that, born in May 1790, he was over four years younger. Now he revealed that he had always imagined *he* would marry beloved Caro. His grief became so hysterical that he had to be given sedation to calm him.[7] Caroline herself wrote him a wistful poem bidding goodbye, as it were, to her girlhood – and his hopes:

> The wand was broke her elves dismiss'd
> The Demons yell'd – the serpents hissed
> The skies were black the thunder roar'd
> When sad Titania left her lord
> And thus in plaints both loud and long
> To stones address'd her mournful song . . .
> Thus spoke Titania then she sigh'd
> Doomed to become a mortal bride[8]

In fact 'sad Titania' and Hart now forged a strong and stable friendship which would prove to be of enormous importance in Caroline's subsequent life. Their correspondence was continuous; there would be incidents in Titania's life as a mortal bride in which Hart, rejected as he might have once been in his own mind, was able to demonstrate his continuing devotion to his wild but charming cousin.

William Lamb was born on 15 March 1779; he was thus six and a half years older than Caroline. He spent much of his youth at Brocket Hall, a delightful country house set on a hill overlooking a river, but at the same time not far from London. After governesses, he was educated at Eton College (where he was a contemporary of Beau Brummell) and Trinity College, Cambridge, before going on to Glasgow University for further education. He then studied law at Lincoln's Inn, and was called to the Bar in 1804. It was understood that all this was leading him to politics – Whig politics of course. Here he was expected to succeed. After all, as the writer Matthew 'Monk' Lewis exclaimed to his mother: '*you know* it would be impossible for William not to do everything better than anyone else'.[9]

All this belies the constant reports of William's 'indolence'. This is not the career path of a lazy young man. Yet it would be remarked upon throughout his life in one form or another. At a moment of exasperation Caroline herself would exclaim to Sydney Morgan: 'His indolence rendered him insensible to everything.' It seems more likely that his privileged but emotionally complicated family background – the rumours, never contradicted, of his Egremont parentage – developed in William Lamb an air of indifference which masked more tumultuous feelings. As time went on self-protection would inspire him to make lightly misogynist entries like this in his Commonplace Book: 'A woman is exactly like a mare; very good to ride, but apt to kick in harness.' Or on the subject of marriage: 'By taking a wife a man certainly adds to the list of those who have a right to interfere and advise him.'[10]

In the meantime, however, it is clear that William fell heavily in love with young Caroline Ponsonby early on: he was enchanted by her. It would prove to be a strong abiding passion. It is not difficult to see why this should be so in the first place. Caroline had an extraordinary charm, from her puckish appearance to her equally puckish behaviour. At the same time high-spirited and in a phrase of the time 'ungovernable', contradictorily, she also loved to learn. There are touching early vignettes of William reading to her, in a fashion that was almost fatherly, certainly protective. And she adored William in return.[11]

At the time, it was the death of Peniston Lamb which set in motion negotiations for a marriage between the Melbournes and the Bessboroughs. Now two formidable women confronted each other. Harriet Countess of Bessborough found a foe worthy of her steel in Elizabeth Viscountess Melbourne. It was once said of the latter that she could not see a happy marriage without wishing to destroy its harmony: this was certainly a prescription for the mother-in-law from hell. Harriet Bessborough did indeed worry – ironic as it might seem in view of her own personal life – about the morals of the family into which her daughter was determined to marry.[12]

Elizabeth Lady Melbourne's father, Sir Ralph Milbanke, had received a baronetcy only after making a fortune, although through her mother she descended from the Earls of Holderness. Married at seventeen, Elizabeth Melbourne was an extraordinary seductive woman, if not a very nice one, as Caroline would soon discover. The reaction of both Melbournes to Caroline as a prospective daughter-in-law has to be described as surly. Lady Melbourne, even at the beginning, never showed the young girl the kind of welcoming warmth, however feigned, which might have been expected from her; Caroline, used to the affection displayed by her own mother, must have found it especially disconcerting. Above all, the two formidable ladies in Caroline's life, Lady Bessborough and Lady Melbourne, neither of whom could be conceivably described as of blameless character, began to snipe at each other. Lady Melbourne for example sneered that she hoped that the daughter would turn out better than the mother (a remarkable instance of the pot addressing the kettle).

Even Caroline's grandmother Lady Spencer, who had been such a strong influence in her childhood, greeted the match with notable lack of enthusiasm.

The wedding of two happy lovers, representing two slightly less happy families, took place in the evening on 3 June 1805 at the house where Caroline had been born, a special licence having been obtained. It was issued by the Archbishop of Canterbury: 'Married by me at the Earl of Bessborough's House in Cavendish Square, London, June 3 1805. James Preedy, Vicar of Winslow.'

The reason for the hurry was not personal: it was to do with the rapidly degenerating international situation as Napoleon Bonaparte extended his martial grip across Europe, which brought a real fear of invasion. The wedding party was strictly limited. Besides the Devonshire House party, the few guests present included Caroline's uncle Lord Spencer and his son Lord Althorp, who had been a potential suitor. Outside however a great crowd assembled undeterred and, in the words of Lady

Elizabeth Foster, who was present with her son Clifford by the Duke of Devonshire, 'by special invitation' of Caroline.[13]

Presents in spite of the limited attendance were lavish: her mother gave her a burnt topaz cross; Little G's husband Lord Morpeth gave a beautiful aqua marina clasp, Lord Melbourne a set of amethysts and Lady Melbourne a diamond wreath. It was her uncle, the Duke of Devonshire, who paid for the wedding gown, while the Duchess presented the veil.

Afterwards there were tales of the extreme nervousness of the bride, some of them told later by Caroline herself. The Duchess of Devonshire did indeed comment at the time to her mother Lady Spencer as to how Caroline had 'crumbled' on leaving her family. Such nervousness was understandable. Lady Elizabeth Foster's account was slightly different: the day before the wedding 'Caroline Ponsonby looks prettier than ever I saw her. As to the wedding, sometimes she was very nervous but in general she appears to be very happy.' Above all, the bridegroom William's manner had been 'beautiful, so tender and considerate'.[14] After the wedding the couple departed for Brocket Hall for a fortnight's honeymoon.

It was the extreme youthfulness of the bride's appearance which caused comment. Even Caroline's own mother observed that she looked 'so unlike a *wife* . . . much more like a School Girl'. A letter from Lady Elizabeth's son (by her actual marriage), Augustus Foster, vividly expressed the contemporary reaction to Caroline's change of status. Foster was in Washington; informed of the wedding by his mother, he wrote back in July: 'I cannot fancy Lady Caroline married. I cannot be glad of it. How changed she must be – the delicate Ariel, the little Fairy Queen become a wife and soon perhaps a mother.' Now, he reflected, she was 'under the laws of a Man. It is the first death of a woman.'[15]

Augustus Foster was wrong. Or he appeared to be wrong. In spite of this dolorous prediction, a time of great happiness ensued – married happiness. In Society something of Caroline the ingénue remained, as demonstrated by a story of her playing the fashionable game Loo (a form of Whist). She got into trouble for not playing out her Trumps. As Lord Henry Seymour remarked:

'she must play one if she had one in her hand although it might prove her own perdition'. Words and tempers flared: Caroline felt frightened as they all turned on her with the contemptuous question as to whether she had ever played Loo before.

'Yes, at the Princess's last night.'

'And what sort of Loo was that?'

'A very different one.' When taxed as to how it was different, Caroline gasped out: 'A much quieter one.' At which everyone fell about laughing and she was restored to favour.[16]

William's political career made a satisfactory start when he was elected MP for Leominster, in Herefordshire on the borders of Wales, in January 1806. He then moved to another constituency briefly, ending at Portarlington, where he held the seat for five years. It was true that there were financial problems.* Lord Melbourne pointedly paid William – his newly established heir since the death of Peniston – a substantially smaller allowance than had been given to the elder boy: an indication of his dubious paternity. On the other hand, apartments at Melbourne House were offered to the young couple.

Melbourne House† was one of the most beautiful houses – palaces is a better word – in early-nineteenth-century London. Built by James Paine in the 1750s, it had been altered by Henry Holland for the Duke of York. Lord and Lady Melbourne moved there in 1793, twelve years before their son's wedding, swapping it with the Duke for their own house. The entrance was in Whitehall, not far from the Houses of Parliament, an even shorter distance from the Downing Street residence of the Prime Minister. The house itself was set back from Whitehall, looking over St James's Park and the Horse Guards Parade, once

---

* MPs received no payment at the time; the first Parliamentary salaries were paid in 1911.

† The name of the second Melbourne House was changed to Dover House in the nineteenth century when Lord Dover bought it from Lord Melbourne; it is now the Scotland Office. The original Melbourne House is known as Albany.

the tiltyard of Henry VIII. A rose garden lay directly behind the house with a gate to the Parade.

Caroline now found herself in the centre of London in every sense. As she told Sydney Morgan in 1811 (when there was some confusion about street directions): 'My direction is always Melbourne House.'[17] But she was also closely juxtaposed to her new family, headed – whatever the social conventions pretended – not by Lord Melbourne but his formidable wife.

The ground floor of Melbourne House was occupied by the Melbournes themselves, and above them loomed a neo-classical rotunda designed by Henry Holland, incorporating the original staircase. This led to the state rooms, all with magnificent views. On the second and upper floors now lived William and Caroline Lamb; access was by a smaller spiral staircase. It will be obvious that their lives were not particularly private, quite apart from the traditional gossip of servants. Caroline's large bedroom, with its lofty alcove containing a large bed, had perhaps the most beautiful view of all, high up over St James's Park. So Caroline was free to receive, to go out, to lead the enjoyable life of a young married lady of fashion – bearing in mind that it was all to be under the watchful eye of her mother-in-law.

All accounts at this point depict a thoroughly engaging young couple. (Harryo had remarked very early on that they seemed 'mutually captivated'.) There is a touching vignette of the two of them closeted in the same chair – a 'tither tother', as swing seats were known – reading appropriately enough a book called *Tales of Wonder*. On another, later occasion, Caroline wrote in bliss to Little G about the first time she went out shooting with her husband: 'It was pretty to see the Dogs and my beautiful husband with all his black hair over his brows and a great colour from the eagerness and animation he felt pacing all over the stubble fields, with his gun on his shoulder and me on his arm.'[18]

Even the slight jealousy she openly felt about an earlier attachment William was supposed to have had to Little G herself, pointed to her own feelings for him rather than anything more serious on his part.

From the first Caroline took her responsibilities as being married to a man with a career seriously. She vowed to be 'silent of a morning – entertaining after dinner' (the former probably more difficult for Caroline to achieve than the latter). She asked her mother's help in order to understand better what William read to her: 'oh, those Lambs, how they do enlighten one's mind,' she cried. So would Lady Bessborough write down relevant events and dates in history? In the meantime her correspondence continued to be littered with references to her reading, a great deal of it historical. On one occasion she excused herself for a delay in writing to her mother: 'I have been really so occupied with the sorrows of Mary Queen of Scots . . . I had always seen the other side, except in Hume, & was surprised at the conviction Robertson seems to carry on every line of her' – a reference to William Robertson's *History of Scotland*. On another occasion: 'we have all been reading a book by Madame de Genlis, *La Siège de la Rochelle, ou le malheur de la conscience*' which she described as 'almost more interesting than any book I have ever read' even if the style was dull.[19]

Caroline's letters to William, her 'Dearest Mannie', on the other hand, are ecstatic as are her various reports to friends and relations. 'I have married not a man but an Angel . . .', she wrote to her cousin Georgiana Morpeth a few months after the wedding; 'take from him his beauty (which by the way increases every day) his being the cleverest and most sensible of all men and yet I say if you look over the whole world you will never find his fellow – he is kinder more gentle more soothing more indulgent talks nonsense better and coaxes me more than a woman could and with all that he is in short perfection'. To Georgiana she added that when William had left her for two nights for a yeomanry dinner, 'I did not know before how cold and melancholy it was to sleep by yourself . . .'.[20]

1806 was marked by a tragic event in Caroline's immediate family. Georgiana Duchess of Devonshire, whose health had been decreasing by painful stages, died on 30 March. The *Morning Chronicle* marked the occasion with a fitting tribute: 'For no less than 33 years have we seen [her] regarded as the glass and model of fashion, and amidst the homage which was paid to her, she moved with a simplicity that proved her to be unconscious of the charm which bound the world to her attraction.' Among the mourners was her friend – and the long-term mistress of the Duke, mother of his children – Lady Elizabeth Foster. Her sadness was not assumed. There had been genuine love between them; in any case Elizabeth Foster's position in Society had inevitably changed. It was presumably according to the wish of the widowed Duke that Lady Elizabeth now took on the role of hostess in his household, whereas the obvious candidate was Harryo, his unmarried daughter. As Harryo told her sister Little G: 'Lady E.F. is very disagreeable in doing the honours instead of me.'[21]

On the glorious occasion of William's first speech in the House of Commons on 19 November 1806, it was natural for his wife to wish to be there to applaud (silently) her 'Dearest Mannie'. William was to make the loyal address to the King at the Opening of Parliament, a signal honour for a new MP, no doubt due to his family connections. At this point the government of England was in the hands of the so-called Ministry of All the Talents: William Pitt had died in January. With the country at war with France, in February Lord Grenville managed to briefly join together Tories and flamboyant Whigs such as Charles James Fox. Lamb himself was not a natural speaker, as he admitted later: 'I was always nervous and I was too vain to expose myself to what I considered the disgrace of speaking in a hesitating manner,' describing his own speeches as 'bothering, tangling'.[22]

At the time Caroline told Little G: 'I only hope he will do it well', although her 'ambitious hopes for his success' were in danger of being destroyed by Napoleon's recent victories in Prussia, ending with surrender by General Blücher.[23] This was a grim period for England: Nelson's naval victory – and tragic death – at Trafalgar a year earlier had been followed by a period when England's European campaigning foundered; Napoleon's on the other hand ascended to new heights. *Le petit bon homme*, as Napoleon had been condescendingly called by the Whigs in Paris during the Bessboroughs' recent visit, was now triumphantly lording it over Europe.

In the House of Commons, women, who were not to be admitted as MPs for over a hundred years, were at this point not even welcomed as spectators in the Strangers Gallery: the only method of viewing proceedings was by an unofficial procedure which was tacitly accepted but was certainly extremely uncomfortable for the ladies who attempted it. 'The Sex', as the term was, could peer down the hole around the lantern which lit the House, otherwise known as the Ventilator; the candles of the chandelier overhead made it unbearably hot as well as producing clouds of smoke.* The Speaker of the House could not be seen, although his bellow of 'Order, Order,' could be heard; the orators – the husbands, brothers, lovers of the peering ladies – could only be viewed by craning the neck.[24]

This was definitely not good enough for Caroline. What was to be done? Showing the defiance of conventions which would become her hallmark, Caroline borrowed some clothes from her younger brother Willy and, with her short hair and slender boy's figure, was able to slip into the Commons unobserved, accompanied by a family friend, a Mr Ross.

Thus she was presumably enchanted to hear William Lamb open the proceedings with a robust speech deploring the gloom cast over the meeting of Parliament by the continuing disturbance of that 'highest tranquillity and happiness' which the continent had once enjoyed. William talked of 'the complete destruction of venerable estates', the fact that the power of the enemy was 'now unlimited over the greater part of Europe'. For peace, it was 'necessary, indispensably necessary' that they themselves should be strong. But William was optimistic: 'We feel the utmost confidence, that, under every difficulty, his majesty will still have the satisfaction of witnessing an increasing energy and firmness on the part of his people . . .'. And so on until he concluded with his confident belief that together they would secure 'the honour and independence of the British crown, and the property and freedom

* In 1834 when, designed by Charles Barry, the Houses of Parliament were rebuilt after a fire a Ladies Gallery behind heavy metal grilles was inserted.

of his brave and affectionate people'.[25] All this was stalwart and patriotic, if not inspired.

Afterwards Caroline was able to return discreetly to Melbourne House, in nearby Whitehall, and change back into her own clothes. Her absence was not of course unobserved by the Melbourne family, to whom she blandly announced that she had been at Lady Holland's in her Kensington abode. The deception was discovered and Lady Melbourne in particular was furious; but the fact was that Caroline, by taking the law into her own hands and using her strangely boyish appearance to her advantage, had managed to do what she wanted – which was to witness William's *début*.

There was a parallel existence to Caroline the adventurous boy-girl: this was Caroline as the mother, or at least future mother. Quite early on Caroline became pregnant with her first child, another happy indication of the success of the marriage. It is true that the spectacle of Caroline, 'the fairy, sprite' in the Duchess's phrase, as a future mother – the ultimate womanly activity for one who still looked like a child to her family – caused a certain amount of amazement.

A letter from Caroline to her 'dearest grand-mama' Lady Spencer, in December 1805 as pregnancy advanced, indicates on the contrary a very cheerful routine. 'Wm. & I get up about ten or ½ after or later (if late at night) – have our breakfasts, talk a little'. Then the reading starts: Bishop Thomas Newton on the Prophecies, later the philosopher David Hume and Shakespeare. William goes for walks and she goes for lesser walks. Caroline adds skittishly: 'Wm. bids me tell you he thinks I am growing quite good. I do not know what to say. I think there is much room still for amendment.'[26]

Unfortunately this pregnancy ended with premature labour on 31 January 1806. William was in his constituency at Leominster but rushed back. Too late. The baby – a boy – died after a few hours and the little body was buried in Hatfield Church, close by Brocket Hall. Such an event, however distressing, was not unusual at the time when antenatal care and care in childbirth were still awaiting the advances of Victorian times. By November

Caroline was pregnant for a third time. The result was the birth of a large, apparently very healthy boy on 28 August 1807, only just over two years from the date of Caroline and William's marriage.

The boy was named Augustus. For Caroline it was love at first sight: the next great love of her life. As her cousin Harryo exclaimed: 'We hear of nothing but the beauty, strength and size of Caro's boy and her rapture at his birth.' The significant step of motherhood changed her life, as the winsome little page apparently grew up, at least in her feelings for her 'dearest Boy'. But it was a development which proceeded naturally and happily from her affection for her husband. She described her feelings herself in her Commonplace Book:

> His little eyes like William's shine
> How great is then my joy,
> For while I call this darling mine,
> I see 'tis William's boy.[27]

Augustus was from the first a noticeably large baby for such a little woman, and as a result was described as a remarkably fine boy, not only by Caroline but generally. He was christened on 13 October and the Prince of Wales, the future King, stood as his godfather. Lady Spencer made the point that the Prince should choose a suitable name: hence Augustus. Perhaps the unexpected presence of Sheridan, long-term lover of the baby's grandmother, at the christening struck a slightly odd note – he accompanied the Prince, despite having no invitation. But Sheridan attempted to make up for it with some cheerful verses saluting the newcomer:

> May he inherit
> Thy Father's manly sense and spirit,
> Thy Mother's grave and gentle heart[28]

At the time there seemed no reason why this wish should not be fulfilled.

Caroline breast-fed the baby herself, at a date when aristocratic mothers were still accustomed to hand their newborn babies over to wet nurses; while some younger-spirited mothers, following the precepts of Rousseau, were beginning to favour what he described as the natural healthy solution of breast-feeding.* In Caroline's case, a wet nurse was probably introduced to supplement her efforts, but she was still attempting to feed Augustus four months after his birth.

Caroline certainly had no intention of handing over her precious boy to nurses for good. Her brother thought her 'very absurd' with the child, when she rode out on the high road: 'the Horse or Ass (I do not know which it is) led by the page in full dress, the baby on her lap and her maid and the nurses following on foot, and then wonders why the Turnpike men laugh at her!'.[29] However absurd to onlookers at the time, this also emerges as a picture of innocent maternal devotion.

With a husband successfully launched on a political career, an apparently healthy baby son she adored, a place in the grandest Society, surely nothing could go wrong with Caroline Lamb's marriage – or her life? Surely those memories of the fairy, the sprite, Ariel, were now subdued by the conventional picture of a woman of her time. In short, no sensible woman could want more, girlish wand broke, mischievous elves dismissed, than to be a 'mortal bride'.

---

* In 1778 Marie Antoinette, then in her early twenties, shocked her mother the Empress Maria Theresa of Austria by feeding her first child herself.

CHAPTER THREE

What a World

'What a world it is dear sweet boy, what a flimsey patched work face it has – all profession, little affection, no truth'

Lady Caroline Lamb to the Marquess of Hartington,
October 1810

IN 1810, FIVE years after her marriage, Lady Caroline Lamb began to have a very public flirtation with a noted womaniser who had in addition a special position in the Whig world. What had gone wrong with the perfect marriage, the couple who sat on a swing seat together reading *Tales of Wonder*? Years later, William would explain to Queen Victoria that he had been too young – 'no man should marry before he was thirty'[1] – but this can be discounted as the comfortable avoidance of a more penetrating discussion.

The lifestyle, like the marriage, seemed ideal: parties and receptions at Melbourne House, country outings either to Brocket in Hertfordshire or Melbourne Hall in Derbyshire, healthy expeditions to the seaside. Politics and the pursuit of political fame by William – if it was a somewhat languid pursuit – surely provided the serious centrepiece of the couple's life together. Sadly it seemed that Titania was proving herself to be a 'mortal bride', like so many of her relations.

It was true that there was a cloud over Caroline's domestic life, which only got darker as time went on. This concerned the health of her 'dearest boy' Augustus. In April 1808, the child, then about nine months old, seems to have had some kind of convulsion. But such fits were not necessarily a matter for serious concern; for the time being the doctors were reassuring. There began however to be comments within the family about Augustus's lack of progress. In November 1807, a few months after Augustus's birth, Harryo had judged three babies in the family circle and pronounced Caroline's to be the finest, with a vivacity which would be rare in a child of a year old. A few months later Harryo gave a very different verdict. Although Augustus was 'the finest, largest, healthiest creature I ever beheld, his face was as far from pretty as possible'. At a year old he could neither speak nor walk, but laughed 'like a lamb and grows en beau and fat': in short a stout and lively child. But the convulsions did not cease. On one occasion Augustus fell on the floor foaming at the mouth.[2]

Inevitably, the Lamb family began to recommend strict nursing, listening to the advice of doctors, maybe even the removal of Augustus from his parents to the care of nurses. With equal inevitability Caroline declined. The passage of time would bring a range of treatments for what appear to have been epileptic fits. While at the same time Augustus continued to be educated, so far as was possible, like any other boy of his age and class. Letters would appear from him, to his grandmother and others; although the text on one occasion looked remarkably like Little G's handwriting, he could undoubtedly read and write for himself as time went on.* Augustus, for example, also went on holiday with his parents like any normal child. On seeing Augustus arrive at Ryde in the Isle of Wight with William and Caroline around the time of his second birthday, Lady Sarah Spencer, a young cousin, found nothing wrong with Augustus's appearance. She

---

* There have been various medical studies of the case of Augustus Lamb, notably Hilary Dickinson, 'Accounting for Augustus Lamb', *Sociology*, Vol. 27 which suggests that although he had learning difficulties, his impairment was milder than the words 'mentally handicapped' indicate.

worried instead whether the Lambs would find Ryde dull after Cowes, where they had been living 'almost a London life' with the Duke of Gloucester.[3]

In the early years of Caroline's marriage, however, it was significant that her enraptured love of her boy – which never ceased – began to move from being a source of joy to a source of worry. On one occasion when Augustus was three and a half, during her continuous correspondence with her cousin (and wistful once admirer) Hart, Caroline chose to send a rhyming letter on the subject:

> Friend of my heart accept this letter
> The child thank God is rather better
> But spite of doctors' drugs and pill
> Has been most wonderfully ill . . .[4]

At first sight William would appear to have been a great deal less worried than his wife; but to be fair that probably represented the natural emotional difference in the behaviour of a mother and a father; especially a father whose famous indolence might extend to concealing those emotions in the first place.

At the same time Caroline's position in Society in real terms was not quite as delightful as her status – niece of the Duchess of Devonshire, wife of Lord Melbourne's heir, future châtelaine and current lively hostess of Melbourne House – would indicate. In November 1807 the Duke of Devonshire questioned his daughter Harryo on just this point: whether people were prejudiced against Caroline by hearing of her 'oddities'. He then put his finger on it by saying that men liked her a great deal better than women 'and that she is very entertaining'.[5]

There was in fact general agreement about the 'oddities' of Caroline Lamb. In the words of the Duke's mistress, Lady Elizabeth Foster: 'Her child has not cured her of her absurdities.' However these innocent oddities – as they currently were – did show an independence which was rare in a young woman in the world in which Caroline had been raised. Lady Elizabeth, for example, cited an expedition to the theatre where Caroline sat

alone in a box with her page; 'and the first thing she saw was
Lord Egremont in the opposite Box, who must have enjoyed it
much more than the Farce'.[6] It was true that Caroline specialised
in friendly relations with her pages: she took a particular interest
in their uniforms. From the other point of view, she enjoyed, as
has been seen, dressing up as a page, taking advantage of her
slender, boyish appearance; and, as in the case of her sly visit to
the House of Commons to hear her husband speak, the conventional uniform gave her the freedom to achieve something which
would have been otherwise impossible.

This was innocent fun. But there was another side to the Whig
world which may or may not have been fun, but was certainly not
innocent. It was impossible for someone like Caroline who had
grown up in it to be unaffected by it. To take the most flagrant
example close to home: the morals of both Caroline's mother
Lady Bessborough and her mother-in-law Lady Melbourne, to
say nothing of the morals of the men who were their lovers,
had, as has been seen, led to a plethora of 'Children of the Mist',
the delicate term for illegitimate offspring. But they were very
far from being the only ones with that misty cloud around their
reputation. Respectability was certainly not the quality which
enabled you to shine in the Whig world. The most fashionable as
well as highly political Whig salon, for example, where Caroline
loved to go, was at Holland House under the auspices of the
awesome Lady Holland, herself not received at Court.

This was because Elizabeth Vassall, then married to Sir Godfrey Webster, had proceeded to capture the heart of the young
Henry Fox, Lord Holland. He addressed her poignantly: 'All eyes
are Vassals: Thou alone a Queen.'[7] The result was a divorce, at a
time when such things were rare – and ostracism from the Court.
But Lord Holland's 'Queen' had her own reign at Holland House
in Kensington.

Holland House had been bought by the first Lord Holland in
1767. Kensington was then on the outskirts of London with 'fresh
air, verdure and singing birds', in contrast to the smoky, grimy
capital. Because of the distance, guests often spent the night after
dining, with obvious possibilities for the increase of intimacy.

Caroline Lamb was immediately intrigued by the Holland House set, to the extent that in December 1806 Lady Spencer expressed concern to her mother: 'When does Caroline come back from Holland House? It is not a good place for her to frequent if it could be avoided.'[8] There was however more to Holland House than the politics – or for that matter the gambling to which the Fox family was addicted. Writers found in it an exciting centre of literary patronage, something which from the first appealed to Caroline as much as the waves of political intrigue. And quite apart from the fascinating Lady Holland, she enjoyed a merry friendship with Lord Holland, celebrated in what Caroline aptly termed 'doggerel rhyme'.

> I am at home with William Lamb
> And he I think is rather better
> He says he does not care a d—n
> Whether I prate or write a letter

In addition to the notionally dissipated Holland House, the devoted grandmother also worried about Caroline's nervous attacks: 'I dread them becoming habitual. I think the physicians (not you) should tell her that much might be done by her trying to resist them. This will be of the greatest use in hysterical complaints, but I do not know whether it will have any effect in fainting & giddiness.'[9] Within the family however Caroline maintained her reputation for the kind of light-hearted episodes which, in contrast to the nervous attacks, made her company prized.

Lady Elizabeth Foster was the target of one such episode. Caroline shared with Little G and Harryo a mischievous attitude towards her. There was Harryo's depiction of Lady Elizabeth's reaction to the death of Admiral Nelson at Trafalgar: 'She sobs and she sighs and she grunts and she groans and she is dressed in black cockades with his name embroidered on every drapery she wears . . . whilst she is regretting she could not have died in his defence, her peevish listeners almost wish she had.' She wrote to her sister in that private Devonshire House language the girls shared: 'I should ask Papa for a frank for our two letters – only Lady Liz will want it, and if we do, my dear 'ady 'iz may chance to give us a spinkum spankum over her knee.'[10] Matters were different now that the spinkum spankum might take the more worldly form of an unpleasant social life with Harryo's stepmother in charge.

In October 1809, the Duke of Devonshire regularised his marital situation – three and a half years after the death of Georgiana – by marrying Lady Elizabeth. The attitude of the girls had always been different from that of the ever-amiable Hart; Caroline accused him of being seduced by 'the wiles of a serpent', to which Hart replied indignantly: when had she ever seen him fawn on 'that crocodile'?[11] The truth was that Hart's position as a bachelor was quite different from that of an unmarried girl.

It was in fact to be a short-lived marriage – the Duke himself died in July 1811 – but it had a marked effect on Harryo in persuading her to change her own state. As the unmarried daughter she might have expected to sit at the head of the table after her mother's death; now Elizabeth took her place. Her marriage to none other than Lord Granville Leveson-Gower, lover of her aunt Lady Bessborough and father of her last two children, followed.

Caroline also saw an opportunity of a different sort. She drew a witty historical parallel between Lady Elizabeth's marriage and the secret marriage of Madame de Maintenon (*Madame de Maintenant* as she was nicknamed – Madame of Now), the confidante and mistress of Louis XIV, whom he finally married after the death of his Queen. A few weeks after the Devonshire wedding, according to Harryo, in front of the assembled family including Elizabeth, now Duchess, and her parents, Caroline began 'reading *out loud* [Harryo's emphasis] a letter of Madame de Maintenon, in which she excuses her conduct towards Louis and says, "*si je ne vais dans sa chambre, à qui pourrait il confier ses secrets*" [if I did not go to his room, to whom could he confide his secrets]'. Caroline accompanied this by describing a series of short scenes which were 'like what we are so often witnessing'. The result was all sorts of loaded questions as to whether Madame de Maintenon was right to behave like this, 'whether she was ambitious or only making generous sacrifices etc.'. Harryo added with regard to her father's new bride: 'I fancied Lady E. was embarrassed' – which no doubt was Caroline's intention.[12]

The wedding of Lady Harriet Cavendish and Lord Granville Leveson-Gower took place on 24 December 1809, roughly two months after her father's second marriage. Caroline was not invited, which annoyed her. Presumably this was because of the embarrassing family connection (obviously Harriet Bessborough's daughter had known Granville in intimate situations since child-hood). 'My dearest Hartington,' Caroline expostulated a few days later: 'Nothing but a long expressive letter from you can remove the affront I labour under at being excluded from my own cous-in's wedding . . . pray send me a favour & cake . . . Send me an account of the ceremony, no soul writes me word what happened, who was affected, how Lord G. behaved, if Harryo was unhappy, how she was drest [sic], what she wore . . .'.[13]

It was now time for Harryo to assume the role of a diplomat's wife, for which she proved supremely suitable with her natural intelligence and her strength of character, forged in a complicated if luxurious upbringing. As such, she would earn the fulsome praise of the diarist Charles Greville for having 'a great deal of genius, humour, strong feelings, enthusiasm, delicacy, refinement, good taste . . . a bonhomie which extends to all around her'. Her role in her cousin Caroline's life was however not quite so simple. Harryo was a strong force – but a critical force. A few years later she would implicitly admit the charm of Caroline's actual presence, by drawing a sharp distinction between her feelings when they were together and when they were apart.[14]

As time went on, it was Hart, still unmarried (although at nineteen regarded as of marriageable age), who became Caro-line's close correspondent. Their letters show a mixture of affection and affectionate teasing, with an additional constant fear on the part of Caroline that Hart would forget her: it is clear that Hart became a kind of rock in her life, and as time would show, a solid rock indeed. He even prescribed remedies for her for a hangover following a riotous party given by the Prince of Wales at Roehampton. The result was a typical letter in Caroline's ridiculous mode which began: 'My most sensitive Elixir of Julep – my most precious Cordial Confection – . . . Truly comfortable spirit of Hartshorn, Tincture of Rhubarb . . . it is impossible, my most exquisite medicine chest, for me to describe the potion you sent me this Morning. Prescribe such powders to all who die for love of your Lordship's tricoloured eyes. etc. etc.'[15]

Another letter of October 1810 began by showing concern for the welfare of 'My Dearest Hartington' rather than her own. 'I am really quite uneasy about you hearing from all sides odd tales told about you – some saying you Cough others that you are feverish and in short all agreeing that you are not quite well – now, my heart of hearts, I conjure you on my knees I entreat you if you are not quite the thing to come immediately to Town & any how write to me as I cannot live if I do not hear from you & if you hear I am dead I know well enough you will regret me.' Caroline then described one of her escapades, how she had been 'a little wild – riding over the Downs and about the sands with all the officers at my heels in a way not very decent for one of my Cloth . . .' before reflecting: 'What a world it is, dear sweet boy, what a flimsey patched work face it has – all profession, little affection, no truth.' At least her sweet cousin knew that her faults were on the surface: 'many a fair outside covers a blacker heart'.[16]

It was to Hart, too, that Caroline chose to confide her thoughts on an interesting new subject of discussion. In 1809 Caroline read Mary Wollstonecraft's seminal *Vindication of the Rights of Woman*, first published in 1792. To Hart she wrote lightly: 'I have read Rights of Woman, am become a convert, I think dissipation great folly and shall remain the whole year discreetly and quietly in the country.' More seriously to Lady Holland she would reflect how men – 'these Lords of Creation who trample us underfoot' – were really just as much women's slaves and 'just as little can do without us . . . only like other noble animals, we let them bridle and Curb us for want of knowing our strength'. She criticised less liberal-minded women who did not 'stand up for the rights of our sex & wear our shackles with dignity'.[17] Unfortunately, when Lady Caroline Lamb began her flirtation with Godfrey Webster, it would be possible to argue that she was standing up for the rights of her sex; impossible to make a plausible case for her wearing her shackles with dignity.

In 1810 Sir Godfrey Webster was twenty-one, four years younger than Caroline; he had succeeded to his father's baronetcy when he was eleven. He was the son of Lady Holland by her first marriage, which had ended in 1797 with an action for Criminal Conversation (adultery) against Lord Holland and the payment of huge damages. Young Godfrey Webster was handsome in a swashbuckling fashion. And he had fought bravely as a soldier in Spain. But he was already conspicuous for his female conquests, quite apart from the publicity which must accrue to any son of the great Whig hostess. His lifestyle – gambling as well as women, which meant he boasted of never being in bed before nine o'clock in the morning – was certainly debauched.

Caroline now embarked on a relationship, to use a deliberately neutral word, which by its ostentatious nature was bound to arouse lascivious public comment, disapproval among her relatives and outright anger in her husband's family. Webster and Caroline were seen everywhere together and absolutely no pretence was made at hiding the connection. Caroline would in fact later deny to Lord Byron that it had actually been a full-blown affair (presumably amorous dalliance had not led to actual consummation). Whether it was true or not, the effect on Caroline's world was the same. And it was the effect, we must believe, that she intended. There was of course the inevitable crude reaction of someone like Augustus Foster, son of Lady Elizabeth, who had once fancied Caroline himself: he told his mother that William was a great deal to blame, 'for had he studied a little more Shakespeare's *Taming of the Shrew*, he might have checked her, her disposition being "not naturally wicked"'.[18] Lady Melbourne however flew into a rage, making it cynically clear that in true Whig fashion it was the publicity not the immorality which enraged her: the former was likely to affect her son's political career, the latter frankly not. She threatened social ostracism if Caroline did not break off relations with Webster.

The response of her daughter-in-law was a long and passionate denunciation of the way William had corrupted her. 'My dearest Lady Melbourne. I must indeed have a heart of iron if it was not most deeply wounded and affected by your letter and conversation, by my Mother's sorrow and by the unparalleled kindness and patience of my friends.' Caroline then, solemnly on her knees, called God to witness that she consented neither to write to nor see Sir Godfrey any more but '*in Public* [*sic*] by accident as a common acquaintance'.

She proceeded however to defend herself by describing the 'almost childlike innocence and inexperience' she had preserved till her wedding. At that moment William had called her 'prudish' and saying she was strait-laced, 'amused himself with instructing me in things I had never heard or known', the practice of vices.[19] This ardent defence raises the obvious question: was the real problem with the Lambs one of sexual incompatibility?

It is true that William, by now Lord Melbourne, had in later life an undoubted taste for flagellation – consensual – which was the subject of banter with his intimate friend of later years Caroline Norton. But at this point Caroline Lamb never gave any indication that sex was the problem: her occasional accusations of abuse (never very seriously made, in contrast to protestations about his 'generosity and forbearance') date from much later. It seems more likely that the practice to which she referred was connected to the boyish appearance which was so much part of her charm, and which she in fact cultivated, in other words sodomy (illegal at the time). But it must be stressed that this complaint was being made in self-defence; all the other evidence leads to a happy marital life in that respect, including an anxious enquiry from Caroline to Little G, already a married woman, as to whether it was all right for a couple to sleep together when the woman was pregnant, making it quite clear both what the word 'sleep' stood for, and that she hoped the answer was yes.[20]

It is more likely that the crack in the marriage actually arose not from sexual but from a certain psychological incompatibility. For better or for worse, Caroline Lamb demanded attention: exhibitionist would be a mild word for some of her exploits.

Whatever roots this attention-seeking had in her family – the little girl among three brothers, whose own beloved mother's attention was constantly distracted from her by her love affairs (and illicit pregnancies) – it was the rich, grand and colourful world of Melbourne House and Whig Society which provided the fertile soil that encouraged its growth. This was also the world which Caroline deplored to her cousin Hart: with its 'flimsey patched work face . . . all profession, little affection, no truth'. In a scene reported to John Hobhouse later, Caroline asked her brother-in-law George Lamb at dinner to remind her what the Seventh Commandment was. With typical Whig assurance, Lamb replied: 'Thou shalt not bother.'[21]

Or to put it another way: Caroline was a romantic who believed in romantic love, and romantic love feeds on constant wonder and reassurance. Religion might have helped her cope with this questing and questioning side of her nature; but religion played little part in the Whig circles in which she lived, and certainly no part with the Lambs. In contrast there was William's own detachment, his famous 'indolence', extending to his emotional life. For example, in spite of the public provocation of his wife's conduct, in spite of the loose Whig morals in which he had been raised, there is no evidence at this point that William himself, whose private life later would cause a sensation, had his own lovers.

An anecdote of a husband and unfaithful wife told (in French) by the diarist Greville seems more expressive of his point of view. The wife turns to her husband in bed: 'I have something very sad to tell you . . . I no longer love you.' 'Oh, that will come back,' replies the husband. 'But it's still worse, I love another.' 'Ah, mais cela passera [Ah, but that will pass],' at which point the husband turns away and goes to sleep.[22] In short, William adored Caroline and that was that, despite these ephemeral troubles – cela passera. On the other hand, with Caroline that was never quite that: it seemed as if she could never believe totally in William's passion, demanding perpetual proof. One letter of many symbolised this when, after a period during which she felt they had been 'troublesome to each other', she begged him: 'condemn me not to silence, assist my imperfect memory and occasionally call me friend-girl Darling . . . & all such pretty names as shew great love'. She signed it 'own Queen – Car Lamb'.[23]

The Webster affair, as it played out, did not seem to have much of romance about it; but romantics do not necessarily succeed in their first search. One of Caroline's letters to Webster's angry mother Lady Holland has a ring of truth: 'If you choose to consider me lowered on account of me being a friend of your son whom everybody seems to scout [deride] because he chooses to have an opinion of his own & not to be led as most others are by the oracles of Fashion I am sorry . . . I am not one to be so easily put down.' But she then promises that in future her friendship with Sir Godfrey will not 'go on in any way to give offence'. She ends: 'I am not wicked enough to live with one Man & like another. I am not lost enough to break everybody's heart & my own by abandoning my husband & child.'[24]

In short, Caroline's ready promise of ending it to her mother-in-law and other promises to her family would indicate that she had already made her point by her public flirtation. There was her natural guilt, not only with regard to William but also towards 'my little blooming Augustus' when she looked at him. But despite her resolve, it did not end quite so cleanly as she had vowed.

There were public incidents involving William, as for example on their wedding anniversary of June 1811. By Caroline's subsequent account to Lady Holland, William left a ball 'early', that is two o'clock, reminding his wife, who was waltzing, of the 'vows and protestations' she had made six years earlier. But Caroline stayed another three and a half hours. However, 'as I drove home, my heart reproached me and tho tired to death I could not sleep'. Caroline asked Lady Holland to burn the letter describing it all – as it transpired, to no avail. In another confession to Lady Holland on the subject of her previous infatuation, she wrote: 'My husband is angry with me, I do not wonder.' Her excuse – if it was an excuse: 'I cannot help it . . . my passions have so long been used to master my Reason.' There were more requests for letters to be burnt: 'if either of us should die I shall on my death-bed be miserable for the letter I wrote last night'. Caroline is ready to gallop over tomorrow if Lady Holland will forgive her.[25]

Yet the early happy times of her marriage had also been marked by squabbles with William on which family members commented wearily, without any suggestion that the marriage was in trouble. Harryo, never especially charitable where her exact contemporary Caroline was concerned, recounted one ridiculous dispute over whether her maid Betsey should go to the Priory in an open or closed carriage; it ended with William storming out, threatening to return late, and Caroline going to the play with her cousin, where 'she cooled a little'. A tiff, a cup thrown, even hurled on one occasion, were the price the indolent William paid for marriage to the fiery bride who had been since youth 'the girl for me'.

Returning to the break-up with Webster, there was a little trouble over the presents Sir Godfrey had given Caroline. It was not so much a bracelet with a lock of his hair in it (according to the fashion of the time), but a present she obviously much preferred, a dog. Caroline began by deciding to keep the puppy, but by some evil chance – or was it an omen? – the adorable little white dog proceeded to snap at Augustus, then nearly three, 'while playing and running', although he did not actually bite him. Caroline took the dog for a further walk, whereupon it fell foaming at the mouth in a fit. Caroline, her guilt only increased, rushed home and prayed for forgiveness: 'They think the dog is Mad.' She would now give back the dog. And she tore off the bracelet. To her mother-in-law she wrote: 'till Sir Godfrey returns you shall take care of his presents for me & then return them. God Bless you my Dearest Lady Melbourne.'[26]

Nevertheless Caroline was still seen flirting with Sir Godfrey at a ball in April and at various other social events during the summer. Then family expeditions to Brighton and the Isle of Wight interrupted the social whirl. Finally in September the affair, such as it was, seems to have been well and truly over. Sir Godfrey briefly turned to a political career, elected MP for Sussex at the General Election in 1812. The question remained

lurking of course whether William Lamb's own political career
had been damaged. At least Caroline assured Lady Holland that
she had told William 'the whole disgraceful truth'. She asked her
to write to her and say she forgave her; she was 'very miserable
and repentant'. To Little G on the other hand, while on a country visit in October 1811, Caroline painted a picture of family
contentment (despite there being no dogs): 'Wm Lamb chases
the Fox and pheasants – I ride a great deal and see much of the
Neighbours – Augustus is my bosom friend . . . he is also Wm
Lambs delight – we are united like 3 flames or 3 oaks or what
you will.'[27]

At any rate relations with Webster's powerful mother were
resumed. Caroline's correspondence with Lady Holland now
stressed her intellectual interests rather than her moral failings:
'I read the New Testament in Greek with great success & am
edified by the slow but sure progress I make in that language.'
It was Lady Oxford apparently who had convinced her that 'her
favourite Greek would alone repress or depress the ardour and
activity of my congenial soul'. To Hart at about the same time
she boasted: 'What may seem singular is that I had just written
a Greek letter to my brother in law, it was the labour of a week
& a Chef d'oeuvre – not being a Porson.' (The reference was to
a contemporary scholar of ancient Greek.)

This was a side of Lady Caroline Lamb, an intelligent literary
woman struggling to establish herself as such, which contrasted
with the reckless young girl 'wild-riding' across the Downs; both
were genuine aspects of her character, but according to the contemporary values for women, the wild-rider inevitably got all the
attention – and disapproval.

Meanwhile the face of politics of England was transformed,
in a change which had been boding for some time. The fifth of
February 1811 marked the official start of the Regency of the
Prince of Wales, due to the encroaching madness of George III.
It was a radical step. Subsequently, in March of the next year, an
attempt at bringing about a coalition of liberal Canningite Tories
and Whigs failed. The hard-line Tories, at the time under Spencer
Perceval as Prime Minister, were set in government – as it turned

out for a decade. William Lamb, disappointed in the failure of
Canning, plagued by financial difficulties, decided not to stand at
the General Election in July.

On 9 March 1812 Caroline took a radical step of her own.
She wrote an anonymous letter to a young poet whose work
Childe Harold was the sensation of Society. 'I think it beautiful.
You deserve to be and you shall be happy.' She urged him not
to throw away his talents and 'above all live here in your own
country'.

It was, Caroline said, the first letter she had ever written without her name on it. Although the poet could easily find out who
wrote it, she asks him in fact to burn it immediately, she expects
no less from Child (*sic*) Harold. Yet Caroline the anonymous
writer ends on a very different note: 'though the greatest wish
I have is one day to see him and be acquainted with him'.[28] It
remained to be seen how the author of *Childe Harold* would
react.

Miniature of Caroline with her mother, Henrietta Countess of Bessborough (Anne Mee, 1814)

Caroline, aged 18, with her dogs, from her sketchbook

Lady Caroline Lamb, aged 29 (Eliza H. Trotter, 1814)

Henrietta Countess of Bessborough (Sir Joshua Reynolds, 1784)

Lady Caroline Lamb (John Hoppner, 1805)

Lady Harriet Cavendish ('Harryo'), daughter of the Duke of Devonshire and cousin to Caroline. She married Earl Granville.

Lady Georgiana Cavendish ('Little G'), daughter of the Duke of Devonshire and cousin to Caroline. She married the Earl of Carlisle.

William Lamb, later Viscount Melbourne (Sir Thomas Lawrence, c.1805)

Marriage certificate of William Lamb and Caroline Ponsonby on 1 June 1805 for their marriage on 5 June

Elizabeth Lady Melbourne, mother of William Lamb, which hangs at Melbourne Hall.

Melbourne House looking over St James's Park and the Horse Guards Parade.

Melbourne Hall, Derbyshire

Emily Lamb, sister of William.
She married Earl Cowper and
later Lord Palmerston.

Caroline's cousin, Hart, 6th Duke of Devonshire

Lady Elizabeth Foster (Bess), later Duchess of Devonshire (Sir Joshua Reynolds, 1787)

PART TWO

LITTLE VOLCANO

'Then your heart . . . what a little volcano! That pours lava *through your veins.'*

Lord Byron to Lady Caroline Lamb, 1812

CHAPTER FOUR

The Thrilling Lyre

'Oh that like thee Childe Harold I had the power
With master hand to strike the thrilling lyre'

Lady Caroline Lamb, 1812

T HE YOUNG POET to whom Caroline Lamb wrote her anonymous letter in March 1812 was George Gordon Lord Byron. He was twenty-four years old. A few days later, having received no answer, Caroline wrote again:

Oh that like thee Childe Harold I had the power
With master hand to strike the thrilling lyre . . .

It was significant that this time she chose verse. Crucially it was his poetry which had first attracted Caroline to Lord Byron: here was the master hand at work in the art in which she was a humble practitioner. She was careful to make it clear at this point that she was not offering 'Strong love':

But Admiration interest is free
And that Childe Harold may receive from me.[1]

This was all true and, on the surface, sober. Caroline Lamb did aspire to writing poetry. Lord Byron's poetry was already the focus of admiring attention – and savage criticism from the august *Edinburgh Review*, which was the dark side of that admiring attention. In 1809 Byron hit back with *English Bards and Scotch Reviewers.*

But after that of course there was the young man who actually wrote the poetry, and the whole world it seemed was talking about him as well as his verse. The more Caroline heard, the more she was inclined, by one means or another if letters did not work, to strike up acquaintance. It is clear that by the time she received an invitation to a party at which Lord Byron was to be present, Caroline Lamb had developed some kind of romantic obsession. When she questioned Byron's friend Samuel Rogers about the poet, he was wary enough of Caroline's tempestuous nature to try to put her off with unattractive physical detail. Caroline in effect tossed her head: 'If he is as ugly as Aesop, I must see him.'[2]

George Gordon had succeeded his great-uncle as the 6th Lord Byron when he was ten years old. Byron was himself the only son of (John) 'Jack' Byron Gordon, who added the name of Gordon when he married the heiress Catherine Gordon of Gight. Jack had had a first hasty marriage to Amelia Marchioness of Carmarthen, with whom he had been having an affair; she managed to be divorced from Carmarthen only just in time to remarry before the birth of their first child. A miserable union followed from which only one daughter survived, before Amelia herself died. That daughter, born in 1783, would be Byron's half-sister; she was called Augusta.

Jack Byron's second marriage to Catherine Gordon proved not much happier. Money troubles were unending, and Catherine was further beset by fits of melancholia, which heavy drinking may have alleviated at the time, but did not help in the long run. She ended returning to her native Aberdeenshire, where most of George's upbringing took place; Jack went to France, where he died in 1791. George Gordon inherited not only the Byron title but Newstead Abbey, near

Nottingham, a beautiful house in acute need of repair, and with a great many debts.

He was sent to Harrow at the age of thirteen. Where George, now Byron, was concerned, love was clearly waiting to pounce. There was a passion for a girl called Mary Chaworth (inspiration of an early poem, 'To Mary'), followed more importantly by a series of passions for boys; John Lord Clare was a great love, and there were others. When he arrived at Cambridge, John Edleston won his heart and after his death was the subject of elegies such as:

> Sweet Thyrza! Waking as in sleep
> Thou art but now a waking dream . . .[3]

All this amounted to an ardent and emotional young man, who as time went on wrote poetry which received public attention.

The physical appearance of Lord Byron added to the allure of his image. A portrait of him in his mid-twenties by Thomas Phillips shows his lips as the focus of his face, with 'their curved outline of Greek beauty': these were the words of his friend Thomas Medwin. Then there were his eyes, greyish-brown 'but of a peculiar clearness . . . a fire which seemed to look through the thoughts of others', his hair with its 'natural and graceful curls'.[4]

It was true that Byron was not particularly tall, and had an unromantic tendency to put on weight, which he countered from time to time with a vegetable diet (and two bottles of wine at dinner). Then there was the matter of his club foot. Byron was born with a deformed right foot, causing him to walk on the side of his foot rather than the sole. But this did not prevent him from being physically active: for example he was a notably powerful swimmer, and proud of it. Where women were concerned, where the imagination of Lady Caroline Lamb was concerned, the 'Greek lips' and the 'natural curls' were infinitely more important. And for Caroline *Childe Harold* was more important still.*

---

* Childe was the medieval word for a young candidate for knighthood.

The subject 'of curiosity, of enthusiasm almost, one might say of the moment is not Spain or Portugal, Warriors or Patriots, but Lord Byron!'. So wrote Elizabeth, the new Duchess of Devonshire, to her son Augustus Foster. She reported that *Childe Harold* was on every table, and the poet, with his 'pale, sickly, but handsome countenance', courted, visited, flattered and praised wherever he appeared. 'In short, he is really the only topic of almost every conversation – the men jealous of him, the women of each other.' Byron himself summed it up in the memorable phrase: 'I woke one morning and found myself famous.'[5]

It was after all an irresistible combination, the melancholy, disillusioned yet romantic poem and the romantic man himself who wrote it. Surely in some way he epitomised his own story. The Cantos told of the travels of a once-dissipated man, denied his true love, turning his back on pleasure:[6]

> And now Childe Harold was sore sick at heart
> And from his fellow bacchanals would flee . . .
> Apart he stalked in joyless reverie,
> And from his native land resolved to go,
> And visit scorching climes beyond the sea . . .
>
> His house, his home, his heritage, his lands,
> The laughing dames in whom he did delight . . .
> Without a sigh he left to cross the brine,
> And traverse Paynim shores, and pass earth's central line

In his travels Childe Harold passed through Portugal and Spain, the Ionian Islands and Albania, ending in historic Greece occupied – as the poet lamented – by the Turks:

> Greece is no lightsome land of social mirth;
> But he whom Sadness sootheth may abide,
> And scarce regret the region of his birth,
> When wandering slow by Delphi's sacred side,
> Or gazing o'er the plains where Greek and Persian died.

Byron himself had indeed travelled far in these foreign lands. What more did a girl of spirit like Caroline need to know before determining to pursue the advances she had made on paper? No one – least of all Caroline herself – doubted her courage and her determination where an adventure was concerned. Here was the person who had gone to a masked ball in 'a boys shoe buckles a red Emery wig a boarding school frock so that I looked like a boy dressed up as a girl, & in that character told everyone that I [im]personated Lady Caroline Lamb'. When as a result she had been rewarded by some 'pretty home truths' about the person in question and seen 'who were my friends', Caroline duly slipped behind a curtain and re-entered in a gown and cassock, hidden away for that purpose, in the character of Sydney Smith, and proceeded to impersonate the celebrated 'Scotch Reviewer, a Yorkshire clergyman – a London wit'.[7] Compared to this enterprise, meeting Lord Byron was surely a great deal less complicated.

The party at which Caroline Lamb literally first encountered Lord Byron took place at the house of Lady Westmorland. There was a ball. Byron was surrounded by a flock of women, but Lady Westmorland led Caroline up to him. Whereupon she looked earnestly at Byron – and turned on her heel. It was a dramatic moment. She recalled her thoughts later: 'That beautiful pale face will be my fate.'

In the fullness of time, Caroline's vivid imagination, helped on by that of her fellow novelist Sydney Morgan, would also produce the unforgettable phrase which has echoed down history: her first sight of the celebrated poet had convinced her that he was 'mad – bad – and dangerous to know'. That is to say that Sydney Morgan reported both sets of words in her *Memoirs*, published in the mid-nineteenth century, having been told to her by Caroline some time after the event.[8] The simpler, ecstatic comment is more likely to be what Caroline actually felt in March 1812.

Byron was obviously ignorant of any ominous thoughts in the mind of the mystery girl whom he glimpsed so briefly. What he saw was a little boyish beauty, slender with short curly hair, a perfect heart-shaped face, huge eyes, and soft lips to match – or meet – his own 'curved outline'. With time he would discover the famous soft, low, caressing voice, in the words of Sydney Morgan, by which even her enemies were seduced. But he was intrigued by her behaviour; this was surely Caroline's intention, whether conscious or unconscious – or a mixture of the two. Put together with the letter whose source had by now been explained to him, Byron decided that he wanted to know more. The opportunity came a few days later at Holland House. Caroline was sitting with the host and hostess. Byron asked Lady Caroline straight out why she had avoided him. He received no direct reply – but he did receive permission to call on her at Melbourne House. It seemed that Caroline was about to hear the sound of 'the thrilling lyre' in the palatial home of her parents-in-law.

And Lord Byron did call. He did not come alone. On 28 March 1812 Byron arrived at Melbourne House with the middle-aged poet Samuel Rogers, whose private wealth – he came from a banking family – enabled him to act as patron as well as friend to the Romantic poets; he was also a friend of Caroline Lamb. There was some confusion since Caroline herself had just returned from one of her hectic rides in the park and was expecting only Rogers. But here was the card of Lord Byron. By her own account in a letter, she hesitated: should she go upstairs and tidy herself before confronting him. 'No, my curiosity was too great and I rushed in to be introduced to this portent.'[9] So the first real meeting between Lord Byron and Lady Caroline Lamb took place between the formally dressed poet and a thoroughly dishevelled young hostess; perhaps there was another portent there.*

Thus Lord Byron instigated a period of calling on Lady Caroline, according to the rules of Society. During this time he regularly entered the palace of Melbourne House, ascended the stately staircase to reach the first-floor State Rooms, incidentally

---

* Caroline told Sydney Morgan that when she heard Byron's name 'she flew to beautify herself'.[10] This may be a fantasy: the curiosity which drove her to be introduced first is more characteristic of Caroline.

passing the rooms of Lord and Lady Melbourne on the ground floor. To reach the private apartments of the Lambs it was necessary to move to a small spiral staircase and climb another floor. (It was said that with time a rope was installed to aid the club-footed Lord Byron in his climb.)[11] These included Caroline's huge bedchamber with its beautiful, airy view of St James's Park, as well as the nurseries of Augustus and small servants' rooms – for, paradoxically, there was no real privacy in the grandest houses. This period lasted about nine months according to Caroline's later recollection. Was it a halcyon time? Perhaps. One cannot help hoping so, in view of all that lay ahead.

When Byron returned to Melbourne House a few days later, he bore with him a rose and a carnation. These were presented with the courtly, half-mocking words, 'Your Ladyship, I am told, likes all that is new and rare for the moment.'[12]

Caroline's response on 27 March 1812 was elaborate and of considerable length; it began with a quotation from Hume and ended with a quotation from *Childe Harold*: 'The Rose Lord Byron gave Lady Caroline Lamb died in despite of every effort made to save it; probably in regret at its fallen fortunes. Hume, at least, who is no great believer in most things, says that many more die of broken hearts than is supposed – when Lady Caroline returns from Brocket Hall, she will despatch the cabinet maker to Lord Biron [sic] with the Flower she wishes most of all others to resemble, as, however deficient its beauty, and even use, it has a noble and aspiring mind, &, having once beheld in its full lustre the bright & unclouded Sun that for one moment condescended to shine upon it, never while it exists could think any lower object worthy of its worship & Admiration.' She then maintains that although this sunflower was 'punished for its temerity', its fate was still more to be envied than that of many less proud flowers: 'it is still permitted to gaze though at the humblest distance, on him who is superior to every other . . .'.[13]

The letter ends on a rather less elevated note. There was something else sacred to Lady Caroline Lamb: dogs. Given Lord Byron's beautiful lines on 'the only dog he ever lov'd', how could he censor the whole dog race by the unjust lines in *Childe Harold*:

> Perchance my dog will whine in vain
> Till fed by stranger hands;
> But long ere I come back again
> He'd tear me where he stands.[14]

If these were halcyon times, the term certainly did not apply to Lord Byron's attendance at one of Lady Caroline's famous waltzing parties. Their dispute on the subject of the dance indicated the potential conflict between them, based from the first on Caroline's boldness – or was it her sense of personal freedom? Waltzing would later be described as the only rival to Lord Byron himself during the season of 1812, the year that it was introduced at the fashionable club Almack's. Not only was the waltz seen as a daring innovation, but it also had something defiant, even radical about it. It was after all by origin a German dance, replacing Society's conventional French quadrille. The Hanoverian origins of the Prince Regent (as the Prince of Wales had recently become) inspired him with enthusiasm for it. The waltz could be seen as some kind of protest, to dance it a mildly revolutionary gesture.

There was a rumbustious element to it as well, as witness a report from Spain by Caroline's brother Fred Ponsonby to his mother: 'We had a grand ball the other night – excellent supper. Then waltzing *after* [sic] supper. I got a tumble by sticking my spurs into a lady's gown, and brought half of Madrid down with me.' However, the other partygoers serenely continued their waltz round the fallen bodies 'in rotation'.[15]

Caroline's passion for the exciting, slightly wicked pastime was shared by her cousin Hart; but not it seems by the Duke and Duchess of Devonshire, who forbade it. So Hart joined in organising the fun at Caroline's. Waltzing parties in the great drawing-room of Melbourne House took place virtually every morning, continuing until two o'clock.[16] There might be fifty people there, who would be later restored by a cold collation in a back room. This was an early-nineteenth-century version of the modern workout, except that there was a distinct element to the pastime of waltzing which was less salubrious than sheer physical exercise, quite apart from its Germanic origin.

This was the obvious intimate connection which the waltz brought about between the sexes, the first time in effect that such public contact had been encouraged.

The reaction of Horace Hornam, who saw his wife whirling with a stranger, was not unusual: he bewailed 'poor dear Mrs. Hornam with her arms round the loins of a huge hussarlooking gentleman'. Byron's poem *Waltz: An Apostrophic Hymn* expressed his fear that the dance 'wakes to wantonness the willing limbs':*

> Waltz – Waltz – alone both arms and legs demands,
> Liberal of feet – and lavish of her hands;
> Hands which may freely range in public sight
> Where ne'er before . . .[18]

But there was a subtext to the poet's disapproval. His club foot disabled him from this particular physical activity. Lord Byron could not waltz. And he now forbade Caroline to waltz.

It could hardly be expected that this new flagrant friendship, the talk of Society, would be welcomed by the Lamb family. William Lamb dealt with it in his usual manner, in which apparent detachment may be assumed to conceal greater disturbance. Lady Melbourne employed a different, bolder method of discombobulating her reckless daughter-in-law. She proceeded to develop a relationship – the nature of it was never quite clear – with Lord Byron herself. Although Lady Melbourne might have justified her actions as being in her son's interests, she also derived understandable satisfaction from the homage, as it became, of

---

* The feeling for the special contact offered by the waltz did not go away. In 1945, Clarissa Churchill, niece of the Prime Minister, wrote: 'In the age of sexy modern dances, once one has really waltzed there is nothing like it.'[17]

the celebrated young poet; her jealous dislike from the first of the uppish little Caroline also played its part.

Elizabeth Melbourne was now sixty. If it was true, as was once said of her, that she could not see a happy marriage without wishing to destroy it, here she was arguably setting about destroying a happy love affair. Sixty or not, her allure remained; like Cleopatra, age certainly had not withered her – she had put on weight – but she also retained 'the infinite variety' of the fabled enchantress. The writer Nathaniel Wraxall, an associate of the Prince Regent, who knew her well, referred to her 'captivating manners and conversation, enhanced by coquetry'.[19] Lady Holland in her Journal also described her as 'uncommonly sensible and amusing' before adding the caveat: 'though she often puts me in mind of Madame de Merteuil in *Liaisons Dangereuses*'. She referred to the novel of Choderlos de Laclos, first published in 1782, which made the vicious Marquise de Merteuil the symbol of a seductive intriguer.

Like Lady Holland, Byron found Lady Melbourne sensible: another word for it might have been worldly. He once told her that her conversation was 'champagne' to his spirits. There was also a teasing element in Byron's relationship with Lady M., a conscious wish to shock the world which made it quite different from his relationship with her daughter-in-law.

An extraordinary situation now developed in which Lord Byron called on the delightful Lady Caroline Lamb at Melbourne House; but he also called on her witty and amusing mother-in-law Lady Melbourne – who also lived at Melbourne House. Two letters written to the two ladies on virtually the same date make it clear that there was room in Byron's life for both, certainly in his own opinion. The note to Caroline is one long intimate expostulation, beginning: 'I never supposed you artful, we are *all* selfish, nature did that for us, but even when you attempt deceit occasionally, you cannot maintain it, which is all the better . . . etc. etc.' In the case of Lady Melbourne, he tells her he will have the honour of waiting upon her 'at two or perhaps a little later, as indeed I would have done before had I imagined you wished it. Believe me respectfully yr. obliged Servt. BYRON.'[20]

Caroline's understandably resentful attitude towards this coupling emerges clearly from a letter to Byron about 'Lady M's' impending visit to Brocket. Clumsily Caroline seizes the opportunity to remind Byron of her rival's age as she resolves to behave well, adding, 'if I feel jealous of her I will remember her age and respect her & if she speaks harshly I will recollect my faults and not answer – She has every fine quality – but if I have too much of it I think she is too wholly without sentiments & romance – she also wants that softness which my mother and *yourself* have . . . So now for anguished days again – but I love Lady M & think she has the *law* on her side & therefore I will be very submissive and kind.'[21]

What then of Byron's relationship with Lady Caroline Lamb? It is clear that, unlike with the dissipated Sir Godfrey Webster, Caroline and Byron were lovers. The details would be much disputed afterwards but surviving letters admit of no other interpretation. Caroline Lamb had found the great love, with poetry entwined around its very heart, for which her unfulfilled romantic nature craved. And she had also, equally importantly for her own satisfaction, found a situation with immense dramatic possibilities for the future.

If Lady Caroline was unquestionably madly in love with Lord Byron, then it is equally clear from his surviving letters that Byron was in love with Caroline – for a time at least. He was also exasperated by her. His surviving correspondence hovers between the two. 'I have never knew a woman with greater or more pleasing talents, *general* as in a woman they should be,' he wrote, 'something of everything, & too much of nothing, but these are unfortunately coupled with a total want of common conduct . . . Then your heart, my poor Caro, what a little volcano! That pours *lava* through your veins.' Having written this, Byron in effect takes it all back. 'And yet I cannot wish it a bit colder, to make a *marble slab* of [you] as you sometimes see (to understand my foolish metaphor) brought in vases tables etc. from Vesuvius when hardened by an eruption.'[22]

At which point Byron himself erupts: 'To drop my detestable tropes & figures you know I have always thought you the cleverest most agreeable, absurd, amiable, perplexing, dangerous fascinating little being that lives now or ought to have lived 2000 years ago – I wont talk to you of beauty, I am no judge, but our *beauties* cease to be so when near you, and therefore you have either some or something better.' Compared to this, Byron's own peak of passion, his judgement of later years that 'she gained an ascendancy of me that I could not easily shake off' is chilly indeed.[23] But it does not contradict it.

Here were two passionate people, one married but reckless, the other marriageable and perhaps more reckless than he recognised afterwards. Some scenes evidently took place between the lovers of a romantic, playful nature. There was a mock ceremony of exchanging vows. With delight Caroline saw opportunities for assuming her other identity as a pageboy. On one occasion, when Byron had been asked to a party and she had not, she dressed up as a page and sidled her way into his carriage.

There were arguments, renunciations. On 19 May Byron wrote sternly to Caroline: 'We must make an effort, this dream, this delirium of two months must pass away, we in fact do not know one another, a month's absence would make us rational, you do not think so, I know it, we have both had 1000 previous fancies of the same kind, & shall get better of this & be as ashamed of it according to the maxim of La Rochefoucault.' The particular Maxime to which he referred read: 'There are few people who are not ashamed of having loved when they no longer love.'[24] He announced his intention of going on a country tour.

The next day Byron chose to witness from a rented window the hanging of John Bellingham, the assassin of the Prime Minister Spencer Perceval, who committed the crime from personal grievances to do with the Napoleonic Wars. Caroline Lamb, who strongly disapproved of capital punishment, was also leaving London. As Byron put it to his friend Thomas Moore: 'On Monday after sitting up all night, I saw Bellingham launched into eternity and at three the next day *** [Caroline Lamb] launched into the country.'[25] But unlike Bellingham, both Byron and Caroline came back.

Society, which had once talked of nothing but Byron, was now agog with chatter about Lord Byron and Lady Caroline Lamb. There was certainly plenty to chat about, as the pair pursued their loving but apparently light-hearted course, with many an opportunity for one of Caroline's favourite masquerades. There was for example the interesting question of 'a little foreign page' calling on Lord Byron in his chambers in Albany. Lady Caroline got in touch with Byron's valet Fletcher and asked him to come round and see her at nine o'clock one evening without telling anyone. On return she wanted him to take the little page: 'Do not tell him [Lord Byron] before-hand, but, when he comes with flowers shew him in.' And this was not Lady Caroline herself: of course not. 'Besides, you will see this is quite a child.'[26]

Gifts were exchanged including precious locks of hair: the fashionable keepsake of the moment, as Sir Godfrey Webster had demonstrated with his bracelet. Lord Byron gave her a ring. Early on Caroline sent Byron a lock of hair, 'a relic of Lady Caroline Ponsonby aged 14', as he liked curiosities, adding: 'I request you keep it for her sake.' These were to be of an increasingly intimate nature, which was part of their intriguing charm – exactly where had the little curl originated? The culmination of this kind of exchange came when Caroline sent Byron a lock of hair from the most intimate place of all, with the following explicit covering note: 'I asked you not to send blood but yet do – because it means love I like to have it – I cut the hair too close and bled much more than you need – do not you [do] the same, o pray put not scizzors points near where quei capelli [mass of hair] grow – sooner take it from the arm or wrist – pray be careful.' The heading of the letter might have warned Byron: 'From your wild Antelope'.[27]

During all this turbulent time, the public reaction of Caroline's husband William continued to be curiously indifferent. He had already indicated privately that his opinion of the authority of the husband in marriage had gone down. An entry in his Commonplace Book revealed that before he was married, whenever he saw children and dogs allowed or caused to be troublesome, he used to blame 'the master of it [sic], who might have at once put a stop to it if he pleased'. Since he was married, he had realised that 'this was a very rash and premature judgment'.[28] The kindness of William Lamb – he was unquestionably a very kind man – combined with his tenderness towards his vulnerable Caro met with his cynicism, the famous indolence, and he made no visible protest.

As it was, he had financial troubles on a lifestyle costing considerably more than the £2,000 a year allowed him by his father (approaching £200,000 in modern values) and his political career was not exactly flourishing. He did not accept the Prime Minister's offer to enter his government and in 1812 at the General Election, as has been noted, chose not to stand for Parliament; this was owing to his money difficulties rather than lack of political ambition. As he told Lady Melbourne: 'It is impossible that any Body can feel the being out of Parliament more keenly for me than I feel for myself.'[29] Obviously the gossip about the troubles of his private life was not regarded by his loyal, ever-critical family as helpful; on the other hand this was hardly an age when moral probity was requested of its leaders (or its royal family, given the private life of the Prince Regent). Altogether there appeared to be a general blight on William Lamb of which his wife's behaviour was only part.

It was William's famously worldly mother who brilliantly perceived where not Caroline but Byron, her respectful admirer, might be vulnerable. During the late spring of 1812 a certain Annabella Milbanke was increasingly present at Melbourne House and Brocket Hall. She was the twenty-year-old daughter of Lady Melbourne's brother. The first time Byron saw her, he thought that she was a 'humble companion' because she was 'more simply dressed than the rest of the assembly'. Later Byron would describe her as having a 'placid countenance' with an unexpected 'strength and variety' beneath the demure exterior.

Part of Annabella Milbanke's perfection however was destined to be of great interest to Byron – as Lady Melbourne had been quick to perceive. She was an heiress. Byron's friend Thomas Moore put it crudely but correctly: 'you had better marry her and repair the old place Newstead'. As an heiress Annabella had naturally attracted other suitors; Edward Michael Pakenham, the handsome younger son of the Anglo-Irish Lord Longford, a gallant soldier and brother-in-law of the great Duke of Wellington, was one of them. He proposed to her in March 1812. He was however dismissed for his manners being 'too silken' on the one hand, and rumours of insanity in the Pakenham family on the other.*30

From the first Byron's own 'silken' manners fared better with the demure but critical Miss Milbanke. This did not mean that she was avid to marry him – or anyone at this point. Like Byron himself, she was enjoying her period of social celebrity. 'I am much the fashion this year,' she wrote to her parents, explaining that she intended to give a party at which none of the men could possibly be in love with her. 'Mankind bows before me and womankind thinks me somebody.'31

This was the young woman Lady Elizabeth Foster described to her son, another potential suitor, as 'cold, prudent and reflecting' for all her goodness and amiability. But it was noticeable that Annabella's letters became increasingly full of references to Byron as the spring progressed. At a morning party of Lady Caroline's, she passed her own judgement on him, less dramatic than Caroline's fabled reflection, just as Annabella herself shrank from Caroline's dramatics: 'I think of him that he is a very bad, very good man.' At the same time she found him 'without exception of young or old more agreeable in conversation than any person I know'.32

So this tumultuous spring passed, with Annabella's presence in the Melbourne social circle a definite factor in the relationship between Byron and Caroline. Naturally Caroline could not let matters rest there. The two young women – Caroline was the older by seven years – were totally unalike; cool, prudent

* General Sir Edward Michael Pakenham, as he became, commanding the British forces in North America, was killed in action at the Battle of New Orleans in 1815. It is not known whether in view of subsequent events Annabella Milbanke ever regretted her decision in rejecting him in favour of Lord Byron.

Annabella accused Caroline of concealing her intelligence beneath a childish manner. She also noted sourly that Caroline Lamb was in fact clever in anything that is not within the province of common sense.[33] Caroline on the other hand decided to meet the challenge of Annabella's presence, the obvious danger where the unmarried Byron was concerned, head on, as she preferred to meet challenges.

Annabella was summoned to Brocket to meet Caroline at the beginning of May. Poetry being never far from Caroline's mind, she sweetly or otherwise offered to show Annabella's poems to Lord Byron. The offer was accepted. Byron's verdict came back: it was favourable, certainly more favourable than Caroline had hoped. Only the last sentence gave her the practical comfort she was seeking, and that came at a certain price: 'I have no desire to be better acquainted with Miss Milbank [sic]; she is too good for a fallen spirit to know, and I should like her more if she were less perfect.'[34]

Meanwhile the apprehension of the two families, Bessborough and Melbourne, concerning Caroline grew ever more intense. As early as 10 May Lady Elizabeth expressed the fear to her son that Caroline might flee with Byron to Greece. 'He is going back to Naxos, and then the husbands may sleep in peace. I should not be surprised if Caro William* were to go with him she is so wild and imprudent.'[35]

Elizabeth was right. Byron was living in St James's Street, near Pall Mall. In late July Caroline Lamb appeared at Byron's door, a coat concealing her habitual page's uniform, the clothes she wore for adventure. 'Let us elope,' she said. The music of the thrilling lyre was luring her from hearth and home, from husband and beloved boy.

---

* As Caroline Lamb was nicknamed within the family to distinguish her from Caroline St Jules, whose husband was George Lamb, known as Caroline George.

CHAPTER FIVE

===

That Moment

'What again I promise & vow, that no other in word or deed
shall ever hold the place in my affection which is & shall be
most sacred to you . . . I never knew till that moment, the
madness'

Lord Byron to Lady Caroline Lamb, August 1812

W HEN LADY CAROLINE Lamb arrived at No. 8 St James's
Street she cried out: 'We must go off together. There is no alternative.'[1]

As it happened, Byron and John Hobhouse were just leaving
for Harrow, according to Hobhouse 'to avoid the threatened visit
of a Lady'. As described by Hobhouse in his diary: 'at twelve
o'clock just as we were going, several thundering raps were heard
at the front of the door & we saw a crowd collected about the
door & opposite to it – immediately a person in a most strange
disguise walked up the stairs – it turned out to be the Lady in
question . . .'. Hobhouse decided that if he abandoned Byron
'the catastrophe of an elopement' would be inevitable. And that
would be 'unjustifiable'.

So Hobhouse, with his determined pawky, slightly disapproving face, sat in the sitting room while Caroline pulled off her
disguise in the bedroom, revealing a page's uniform. That would

not do either. Finally she was persuaded to put on a dress, bonnet and shoes belonging to a maidservant in the house. Still the alarm was not over. Seizing a convenient court sword Caroline swirled it about, stabbing into the air as Byron attempted to hold her: 'There will be blood spilt,' she said, and when the two men ignored the threat added, 'Then it will be mine,' trying to stab either herself or Byron and Hobhouse as Byron sought to restrain her.

At last Caroline was calmed. She agreed to go to Hobhouse's rooms to change her clothes. Finally Caroline was persuaded to go back to her own house. But she asked in vain for a private meeting with Byron alone before she departed. Hobhouse refused to relinquish his friend to such a dangerous rendezvous, as he saw it. In this sad way, a bedraggled Caroline Lamb returned to Melbourne House.

At this point things got much worse. Lady Bessborough, whose health was deteriorating fast, was trying to get Caroline to leave London (and Byron). But as accounts of what had transpired reached the Melbourne family – no doubt from Lord Byron to Lady Melbourne – it was Lord Melbourne, not his wife, who made the distraught Caroline lose her head completely. She reported as much to her mother-in-law.

'Lord Melbourne came into my room and said he should tell [William] every thing – & in the most insulting manner assured me Lord Byron would not take me if I wished . . .'. (Lord Melbourne actually said, 'Go and be damned!', before adding that he doubted Byron would have her.) Caroline continued her report to Lady Melbourne: 'In short he [Byron] despised me – as to that I am as sure of Byron as I am of anything on earth – but I will not for worlds involve him in my own ruin.'[2]

But Lord Melbourne had managed to strike the one blow which completely felled Caroline: he suggested that Byron did not actually love her, this epic romance did not exist. Caroline had to believe in Byron's passion or she believed in nothing.

As a result of Lord Melbourne's contemptuous dismissal of this same passion, Caroline then made her own dramatic declaration: 'Forget my existence all of you – I shall instantly set off for

Spain,' where her soldier brother-in-law Frederick Lamb currently was. 'I will behave in no way to disgrace my family & it is but a temporary absence.' She ended: 'comfort my mother' and 'take care of my boy'.[3]

On 12 August Lady Caroline Lamb ran away. Whatever Caroline's wild hopes had been earlier, this was not an elopement. She went alone. It was noon. She ran all the way up Pall Mall, concealed herself in a chemist's shop till she thought pursuit was over, and sold a ring to pay for a Hackney coach. She ordered the man to take her to the first turnpike 'after the stones', that is on the way out of London; whereupon he took her to Kensington, familiar territory from visits to Holland House. Here she borrowed twenty guineas on the pledge of another opal ring: her plan was 'to go to Portsmouth and embarking in the first Vessel that sail'd from there, wherever it might happen to be bound for'.[4]

When Lord Melbourne reported the news to his wife and Harriet Bessborough, together the two 'Queen Mothers' rushed to Lord Byron. They found him 'as much astonished and as much frighten'd' when he heard what had happened as they were. 'He promis'd to restore her if she was to be found . . .'.

Meanwhile her sick mother continued to search desperately, as she confided to her lover, Granville Leveson-Gower, either walking or driving to any place Caroline could possibly be at.

At nine in the evening, the exhausted Harriet Bessborough retreated to the house of her nephew Hart. It was here that news of Caroline at last reached her – and it was Byron who was responsible. He sent a packet of letters from Caroline which had reached him via the driver of that Hackney coach she had hired. Byron then revealed that he had threatened and bribed the coachman until he drove Byron to the house of a surgeon that she knew, where Caroline had taken refuge. Here he managed to force his way in by pretending that Caroline was his sister. Caroline herself had declared that she had run away from her friends and never would return to them.

Byron now brought Caroline to her mother's house. In Harriet's own words to Granville: 'where I am mortified to say – it was more by his [Byron's] persuasions than mine, and almost reproaches at her bearing to see me suffer so much, that she was induc'd to return with me to Whitehall'. Here the Melbournes' welcome was gratifyingly kind, and Caroline appeared much touched by it. William as usual enacted the part of the enigmatic but tolerant husband.

Harriet ended her account to Granville: 'But Oh, G., what will become of it?'[5]

It was now the resolve of Harriet to get Caroline away to Ireland where the Bessborough family estates in Kilkenny would provide, it was to be hoped, an environment free from the glamorous aura of Lord Byron. One element in this determination was certainly Harriet's own sickness: she told Granville she felt very weak and spat a good deal of blood in the night. However she had been given a remedy which was unpleasant but worked: 'And if I can but get her to go I do not mind, and will set out tomorrow.' But in the course of a journey back to Melbourne House to bring this about, Harriet Bessborough seems to have suffered a stroke. She had to be taken back to Cavendish Square. At which point Harriet's loyal long-serving lady's maid, Mrs Peterson, spoke for many in the Bessborough entourage when she denounced Caroline for the effect her shenanigans were having on her beloved mother's health. 'Cruel and unnatural as you have behaved, you surely do not wish to be the death of your mother.'[6]

Certainly the Ponsonby family in general, like the Lamb family, wanted the outrageous Caroline out of the way. It was not so much her immorality as that ungovernable quality in Caroline, so unsuitable in a woman, which assailed their very position in Society. But Caroline herself still prevaricated. Rightly or wrongly, she told her mother she did not want to travel as she might be pregnant. (The possibility that this was true, which was not contradicted by William, would seem to indicate that husband and wife continued to sleep together during this period.) There was after all an undoubted need for a male heir to the title in the Melbourne family; poor beloved Augustus, whose physical troubles continued, was unlikely to be able to fulfil that role;

William's two younger brothers had as yet no children. But the possibility, if it existed, did not become reality.

In the end the expedition to Ireland was agreed.

Byron was informed and, understanding that this was the ending of their relationship, wrote Caroline an intoxicating letter which at the same time has an air of finality: 'My dearest Caroline,' he began, 'If tears, which you saw & know I am not apt to shed, if the agitation in which I parted from you, agitation which you must have perceived through the *whole* of this most nervous *nervous* affair' had not convinced her, together with all he had said and done, and was still prepared to say and do, then he had no other proof to offer.

'God knows I wish you happy,' he went on, 'and when I quit you, or rather when you from a sense of duty to your husband & mother quit me, you shall acknowledge what again I promise & vow, that no other in word or deed shall ever hold the place in my affection which is & shall be most sacred to you, till I am nothing.' Furthermore: 'I never knew till *that moment*, the *madness of* – my dearest & most beloved friend – I cannot express myself – this is no time for words.'[7]

With those magic words, Byron seemed to choke as he wrote. Then he changed his tune. He proceeded to describe his future movements. 'I am now about to go out with a heavy heart, because – my appearing this Evening will keep any absurd story which the events of today might give rise to.'

So Byron had felt '*that moment*' of madness. Undoubtedly Caroline had felt it too. What else but a moment of madness which had led the figure of a little page to appear at St James's Street? She knew it herself, as her letter of penitence to Lord Byron afterwards showed: 'Dearest Lord Byron – be pacified and hear me. I am without excuse . . . I trust myself to your compassion . . . if you tell any one that I attempted to see you I am lost irretrievably lost – if not be quite assured I will neither write nor send nor see you – I really leave London immediately . . . be quite secure that I will intrude no more.' She continued by expressing fears that she had offended him: 'I fear it and this thought makes me most wretched.'[8]

There were many other moments of madness and there would be more in the future. But the question of madness raises the larger issue of Caroline Lamb's whole mental stability. Of course on this subject, as with medical analyses of historical characters generally, there can never be absolute certainty in the absence of the patient; only possibilities which can be raised and probabilities which can be suggested.

It has been seen that frequent gibes had been flung at little Caroline Ponsonby in her youth on the subject of her high-strung temperament. When she was eleven, she had attempted that merry roundelay on the subject to Little G beginning 'I'm mad/ That's bad'. There were tantrums, and there were also outbreaks of high spirits and combinations of the two. The little sprite Caroline famously did not like being thwarted, to the extent that her aunt Georgiana Duchess of Devonshire, echoed by the Duke, feared that any check on her marriage to beloved William Lamb might have led to 'madness or death'.[9]

It is true that the words 'mad' and 'madness' were much used at the time, and thwarted love above all was considered to be likely to produce madness.[10] Stories about deserted women turning to insanity were fashionable towards the end of the eighteenth century and at the beginning of the nineteenth.* Lines from the street ballad 'Crazy Jane' by Matthew 'Monk' Lewis, which was published in his collected poems in this same year of Caroline's attempted 'elopement', 1812, summed it up:

> He seemed true and I believed him
> He was false, and I undone.
> Since that hour, has reason never
> Held her empire in my brain:
> Henry fled: with him forever
> Fled the wits of Crazy Jane!

---

* In 1825 Professor Alexander Morison, President of the Royal Physicians in Edinburgh, in *Outlines of Lectures on Mental Diseases* argued the case that 'Love produces febrile symptoms, and increased sensibility when hopeless – sometimes insanity.'[11]

In the case of Caroline Lamb one modern diagnosis would be that she was suffering from bipolar disorder, formerly known as manic depression. Symptoms include mood swings, agitation, racing thoughts, periods of manic energy – and equally periods of depression. The trouble is that Caroline Lamb, while easily demonstrated as having racing thoughts, manic energy, a conviction of her own ability to achieve anything however improbable, did not, as one authority has pointed out, suffer from corresponding periods of depression.

Another equally realistic picture therefore sees her as highly strung, and above all attention-seeking to an extraordinary degree. A typical glimpse of this is provided by her grandmother's letter of April 1811: 'How is dear C?' enquired Lady Spencer of Harriet Bessborough. 'I have written a few rather serious lines in answer to a letter I had from her which rather vexed me, by telling me she had jumped over a couch at some assembly. Dear child, she does not know how much she lowers her character by such improprieties.' But from Caroline's point of view, she was not so much lowering her character as creating a new and bolder one; just as she enjoyed riding in St James's Park in the early morning 'without husband or father' – another complaint of Lady Spencer. 'Dear Caroline. She fidgets me sadly,' was her grandmother's conclusion.[12]

Whatever the origins of such need for attention, Caroline Lamb, as time would show, wanted to believe. Above all she wanted to believe in love. In Byron, with poetry as his squire, she thought she had found the supreme love. If it was for a moment one kind of madness which they shared, the madness of love, 'that moment' in Byron's own words, then rejection substituted something more like the lack of reason of 'Crazy Jane'. But Caroline Lamb was not crazy: as time would show and the world would discover, she was an unusual, intelligent and independent woman afraid of nothing (except the absence of love).

Harriet Bessborough succeeded in her wish to take Caroline to Ireland at the end of August. The party consisted of the two Bessboroughs and the two Lambs – William accompanied

Caroline, having earlier withdrawn from politics in England, as has been noted, for financial reasons. Parliament was dissolved on 29 September ready for a new General Election, news which reached the Bessborough party in Ireland, but William was out of it. 'It is actually cutting my throat,' he wrote to his mother.[13] Nevertheless he remained at his wife's side.

They arrived at Bessborough House in Co. Kilkenny at the beginning of September. This estate had been granted to a Protestant ancestor, Sir John Ponsonby, by Oliver Cromwell, as part of his conquest of Ireland after his invasion. The seventeenth-century Cromwellian Settlement had led to the triumphant establishment of many similar Protestant families, in many cases dispossessing Catholic inhabitants. As a result the Anglo-Irish aristocracy, the Protestant Ascendancy as they were sometimes known, now presided over a country which was predominantly and ardently Catholic.

Despite this huge majority, in 1812 the Catholics in Ireland, like the minority Catholics in England, had no rights at all: there was as yet no question of Catholic Emancipation. In 1798 a serious rebellion, backed by France, had threatened the whole English regime there. One of the consequences of this rebellion was the Act of Union passed in 1801, which put an end to the independent Irish Parliament. This was the Act which Lord Bessborough had taken 'a decided part against' in the House of Lords, showing a wish to side with his Irish tenants. At one point the prospect of Emancipation had been dangled in front of the Irish Catholic aristocrats as an inducement to cooperate. Finally it was silently withdrawn at the urgent instance of King George III, who saw it as a betrayal of his Coronation Oath (an action that would threaten his fragile mental stability).

Bessborough House was described about this time in a book about *The Beauties of Ireland* as 'a spacious structure of square proportions . . . Viewed as an architectural object, its prevailing characteristic is that of massy respectability.'[14] From the first Harriet Bessborough was determined to strike a similarly respectable note with the tenants, despite her weak physical condition. Some competitive local dancing resulted in a strongly vocal dispute between the Piltdowners and her own villagers, the Carrickers, who 'wore white waistcoats with sashes and bows of Ribbon like the Dresses in a Ballet', as Harriet reported to her lover Granville Leveson-Gower. The Piltdowners declared that they might not be finely dressed 'nor so *Cockaded*' as the Carrickers, but 'they could hollow as loud and fight as long as they could for My Lord and Lady'.[15]

The housekeeper became distressed at the yells sounding more like wild war whoops than anything European: '*Och!* my own dear Lady, there will be *murter* below and we shall all be kilt!' She then asked her Ladyship in her prominent Irish accent if she would make 'a *bet* of a *Spache* off the stage' to set everything right. Harriet not only stretched her 'poor voice' to its utmost pitch in making her 'bet [bit] of a Spache' but ordered great jugs of whiskey punch and, going down among the tenants, took the first glass herself. The tenants were delighted; it all ended with Caroline and the maids joining in, and dancing round Harriet with a garland. Harriet wrote to Granville: 'I shall come back with the brogue I know.' But she ended: 'it gave me a little notion of how hard they are to manage'[16] (underestimating surely the power of whiskey punch).

This was the kind of encounter Caroline thoroughly enjoyed. While at Brocket, for example, she always displayed an enthusiastic wish to participate in village life. In a different way, during the months Caroline Lamb spent in her ancestral Ireland, political events and the political situation left a strong impression on her. If she did not exactly come back with the brogue, in Harriet's phrase, she would demonstrate her interest publicly in an unexpected literary fashion in the future.

For now, her Irish 'exile' included a visit to Lismore Castle, the Irish Devonshire estate, property of her cousin Hart. This was a twelfth-century castle in Co. Waterford, built high above the River Blackwater, which had come into the Cavendish family in the mid-eighteenth century by marriage to an heiress. When Hart inherited it from his father it was in much need of restoration. It was a point made by Caroline Lamb. She was still in constant correspondence with her mother-in-law, in order to reassure herself about Augustus: 'I will you give a kiss & my love to my dear little Boy it is near ten days since I had the happiness of hearing he was well . . .'. But she took the opportunity of one letter to contrast Bessborough in Kilkenny, where everything bore the appearance of 'plenty health cheerfulness & cleanliness', with Lismore. The approach to the castle had been 'dreary . . . solitary'. The interior had been a further disappointment. Here was not a Gothic hall, as she had hoped, but 'two small dapper parlours' much like a villa in Highgate. And it was damp.[17]

On that subject Caroline allowed herself a little fun with the young Duke himself. Her mother described the scene in a letter to Granville, how Hart and Caroline had many disputes on the damp of Lismore. Then one night Caroline suddenly opened the great door of the castle very wide, saying: 'Pray walk in, Sir; I have no doubt you are the rightful possessor, and my Cousin only an interloper usurping your usual habitation.' For a long time nothing happened, and then at last, 'with great solemnity and many pauses, in hopp'd a *frog*'. Caroline followed with two candles, so as to 'treat the master of the Castle with proper respect', she said.[18]

Perhaps Caroline's mockery helped persuade Hart 'the interloper' to transform Lismore into a romantic Gothic fortress, unfit for a frog. The architect William Atkinson spent the next ten years carrying out work at Hart's request: the result was a magnificent tribute to what he described to his sister as his own 'princely power of doing good'.[19]

Throughout the visit to Ireland, beneath this characteristic endearing frivolity, there was an air of thwarted passion about Caroline Lamb.[*] She did not outspokenly declare her continuing love for Lord Byron. Her constant theme in her turbulent letters to Lady Melbourne was rather different: Byron had definitely

---

[*] The phrase was used by the novelist Anthony Powell in *The Valley of Bones*, part of the great sequence *A Dance to the Music of Time*; his narrator Nicholas Jenkins discovers 'Lady Caro's Dingle' in the glade of a park which she visited at this traumatic time and senses 'an air of thwarted passion' haunting the grass-grown paths and ornamental pools.[20]

once been in love with her. Since Lord Melbourne crudely suggested otherwise, causing her to stage that dramatic if short-lived disappearance, this had become an obsession.

In the meantime Byron himself, in his own similarly long-winded correspondence with Lady Melbourne, was displaying a very different approach. On 12 September he raised the one obvious solution to the Caroline Crisis: marriage to another woman. But along the way he hinted at something else: 'Now my dear Ly. M. you are all out as to my real sentiment – I was, am, & shall be I fear attached to another, one to whom I have never said much, but have never lost sight of.' (This was presumably a reference to his half-sister Augusta Leigh.) He then passed on rapidly from that hidden and perhaps now remote passion to a more practical expedient: 'there was & is one whom I wished to marry, had not this affair intervened, or had not some occurrences rather discouraged me . . . As I have said so much I may as well say all – the woman I mean is Miss Milbank[e] . . . I never saw a woman I *esteemed* so much.' And esteem and confidence was surely a better basis for marriage than romance. But an approach to Annabella Milbanke on the subject from her aunt Lady Melbourne received for the time being a cautious negative.[21]

At this point there was introduced a third element in Byron's rich if convoluted personal life: he began having an affair with the mesmerising courtesan Jane Harley Countess of Oxford. The daughter of a Hampshire vicar, Lady Oxford was summed up by the diarist Thomas Creevey as 'a very beautiful woman . . . of indifferent reputation'; her lovers included the King's son, the Duke of Cumberland. Byron felt himself very much at home in her country house, Eywood in Herefordshire: it was not only what he called the 'autumnal charms' of Lady Oxford herself – she was nearly forty, sixteen years older than Byron himself – but the delight of her family life. Known as the Harleian Miscellany on account of their dubious paternity, her children included the delightful eleven-year-old Lady Charlotte Harley, to whom Byron took a sentimental fancy.[22] The omens were not good for Lady Caroline Lamb.

Already in Ireland she began bombarding Byron and even Lady Oxford herself with letters sent directly to Eywood. Byron responded on one occasion with a letter bearing the seal of Lady Oxford – a deeply hurtful move, which was surely intentional. The text of one letter could hardly have been more wounding – or more direct: 'Lady Caroline – our affections are not in our own power – mine are engaged. I love another . . .'. Byron went on to reproach her for 'your Levities your caprices & the mean subterfuges you have made use of while madly gay . . . I am no longer yr. lover – I shall never be less than your friend – it would be too dishonourable for me to name her to whom I am entirely devoted and attached.'[23] This searing message had in one sense the appropriate effect of convincing Caroline 'that moment' had certainly passed; but Byron did not foresee the use that his discarded love would make of it in the future.

There were complicated exchanges of letters between Lady Bessborough, Lady Melbourne and Byron on the subject in which promises were made that letters would be destroyed (and not always kept). Byron told Lady Melbourne: 'If C makes her debut here [Eywood] we shall have a pretty scene!' He added: 'she requires FRIENDSHIP but you know with her disposition it is impossible'. It was a judgement with which Caroline, if she had been honest, would probably have agreed; but at this point friendship was not what the little volcano, as Byron had once tenderly described her, was after. On 21 December 1812 he made a very different comparison: 'perhaps in the year 1820 your little Medea may relapse into a milder tone'.[24]

Caroline Lamb returned to England from Ireland with her mother at the end of November. Her physical appearance did not make a good impression on her cousin Harryo. Whereas Lady Bessborough appeared 'stout and well', as Harryo told Little G, and William Lamb 'laughs and eats like a trooper', Caroline seemed worn to the bone, pale as death, with her famously huge eyes 'staring out of her head'. She was alternately 'in tearing spirits and in tears'. But then Harryo was always a biased commentator where Caroline was concerned, suffused with jealousy from childhood onwards. She herself analysed her complicated reaction to her cousin: 'I hate her character, her feelings and herself when I am away from her, but she interests me when I am with her . . .'.[25] At the end of 1812, the year that had brought 'that moment' to Caroline, and in a different way to Byron, it was not at all clear what interesting course her future life would take.

It then did become rapidly clear that this future life was unlikely to include Lord Byron, except in such a tempestuous fashion that Caroline's fragile sanity would be in danger. Caroline showed her recognition of this in her own style at Brocket during the Christmas season. She organised a bonfire for the villagers; amid the burning logs and branches were tossed by dancing village girls apparent relics of Lord Byron, presents, letters, trinkets and the rest. An actual effigy of Lord Byron replaced the Guy Fawkes of those traditional bonfires on 5 November. It was said that to make it quite clear who was involved, they also wore buttons inscribed *Ne crede Biron*, a mockery of the poet's official motto *Crede Biron*.

One of Caroline's beloved pages was instructed to recite the poem she wrote for the occasion:

> Burn, fire, burn, while wondering boys exclaim,
> And gold and trinkets glitter in the flame
> Ah, look not on me, so grave, so sad.
> Shake not your heads, nor say the lady's mad . . .
> Young tho' I seem, I leave the world for ever,
> Never to enter it again, no, never, never![26]

But whatever Lord Byron and others may have hoped for in a fit of exasperation, Lady Caroline Lamb was not about to leave the world forever. The question for the future – her future, William Lamb's future, Augustus's future, and to a certain extent the future of Lord Byron – was how Caroline would deal with a situation in which one option was evidently despair.

CHAPTER SIX

Ye Dagger Scene

*'It was at this ball that Lady C. L. performed ye dagger
scene of – indifferent memory'*

Note by Lord Byron

UNFORTUNATELY FOR HER family, the little volcano which
was Lady Caroline Lamb showed no signs of being extinguished
on her return to England. If the bonfire at Brocket had indicated
some kind of farewell to Lord Byron, two daring, not to say
outrageous actions on her part at the beginning of 1813 gave the
opposite message.

In early January she boldly turned up at 50 Albemarle Street,
the Mayfair office of John Murray, Byron's publisher. Murray,
now in his thirties, had inherited the business from his father
when he was only fifteen; he had from the first shown extraordinary enterprise in his ventures. It was Murray who had shared
in publishing Walter Scott's *Marmion*, who had launched the
Quarterly Review, and in 1811 he published the first two Cantos
of *Childe Harold*. His house at Albemarle Street rapidly became
a focus of literary London. Caroline purported to bear with her a
letter from Lord Byron, entitling her to choose a portrait – 'which
Picture you think most like' – provided she subsequently returned
it.[1] There was a scrawled signature.

Murray was convinced. Lady Caroline had her picture.

She had in fact made several efforts to acquire a portrait, in particular that miniature by George Sanders done in the past year. Perhaps Byron's friend Lord Clare could obtain the picture and then pass it on to her? Clare refused. The artist also refused. Caroline then openly announced her intentions to Byron himself – to his horror.

Afterwards Byron, not for the first time, poured out all his indignant feelings on the subject of Caroline to Lady Melbourne – 'Such is the reward of returning a woman to her family.' In other words, he had restored her 'effigy' after she ran away; she should now return his.[2] Byron besought Lady Melbourne to speak to her daughter-in-law and make her see reason.

To John Murray he explained that he had been 'imposed upon by a letter forged in my name to obtain the picture left in your possession – This I know by confession of the culprit, & as she is a woman (& of rank) with whom I have unfortunately been too much connected you will for the present say little about it . . .'.[3] And he urged John Murray to demand a seal as well as a signature before handing over anything of Byron's in future. But he did in a sense have his revenge.

Throughout this period, Byron's relationship with Lady Oxford, enhanced by his affection for little Charlotte Harley, was flourishing: he gave her a ring and other trinkets that Caroline Lamb had given him. To Lady Melbourne, who could be counted on to receive any malign snippet about her daughter-in-law with glee, he confided: 'I mean (entre nous, my dear Machiavel) to play off Ldy O against her [Caroline].'[4] And he had not given up on the prospect of an advantageous marriage to that demure and fascinating heiress Annabella Milbanke.

This explains, if it does not exactly excuse, his move when Caroline, still lost in memories of 'that moment' now increasingly far away, asked for that traditional keepsake, a lock of Byron's hair, to replace the miniature; he did indeed despatch a lock – but it was in fact the hair of his mistress, Lady Oxford. There could be no cruder dismissal of the romantic hopes of Lady Caroline Lamb.

Caroline's next daring move was to have a dramatic literary sequel which she could hardly have anticipated. She managed to make one of her entrances – this time into Byron's new lodgings, where he had moved from St James's Street in January; these were at 4 Bennet Street, just off Jermyn Street. Finding Byron absent, Caroline wrote: 'Remember me!' in a copy of his novel *Vathek*.[5] The answer, apparently written down by Byron in a passion when he returned, with its terrible last line, echoes down history:

> Remember thee! Remember thee!
> Till Lethe quench life's burning stream
> Remorse and shame shall cling to thee
> And haunt thee like a feverish dream!
>
> Remember thee! Aye, doubt it not.
> Thy husband too shall think of thee:
> By neither shalt thou be forgot
> Thou false to him, thou fiend to me!*

Finally Caroline did secure her meeting. On 29 April 1813 Byron, having established that Lady Oxford did not object, agreed. He did not however hold out any hope of a return to romance; his tone was noticeably tart: 'You say you will "*ruin* me". I thank you but I have done that for myself already; you say you will "destroy me", perhaps you will only save me the trouble.' Yet in spite of Byron's resolutions, it is possible that towards the end he weakened, and that Caroline's account much later contained the truth: 'he asked me to forgive him, he looked sorry for me; he cried'.[7] After all, he had loved her once.

Throughout all this time, Caroline had one anxiety which did not change. The role of mother was a perpetual source of stress.

---

* The poem was only published after Byron's death. A Byron scholar has demonstrated that the poem had been revised: the familiar version is shown here, ending with the crucial line '*Thou false to him . . .*', whereas in the unrevised version it ended the first verse.[6]

During her enforced absence in Ireland, Lady Melbourne, the grandmother, was peppered with enquiries about her 'beloved boy'. At the beginning of 1813, with Caroline back in England, Augustus Lamb was five and a half. The large baby had grown into a sturdy little boy of significant strength which sometimes added to the problems of controlling him. At the same time Caroline's little sketches show a figure of considerable charm – at any rate in his mother's version. And there were moments of fun, as for example in August 1814 when Caroline rode over to Hatfield from nearby Brocket, as she loved to do, accompanied by Augustus. When they arrived, they were graciously received by the Marquess of Salisbury; at which Augustus, instead of bowing according to custom, knelt before his Lordship. As Caroline told her mother: 'it looked very comical'.[8]

But the health news was basically not good. Lord Salisbury was presumably gratified by the obeisance; less happy were servants jumped on in the course of jollities, or crashing into the snow from an upturned sledge. Augustus grew larger and he was boisterous. The fits continued. Nowadays Augustus's general condition would probably be described as autistic. From the first he found difficulties in talking, understanding and expressing himself: the lack of communication skills, both verbal and otherwise, that are the mark of autism. If Caroline Lamb is accepted as bipolar or manic depressive, then this condition might have affected her son's autism, although there can be no certainty in either case.

There is also an association between autism and epilepsy. It has been suggested that this epilepsy was the result of an unsuspectedly close relationship between Caroline and William – the former as the secret child of Charles Wyndham, one of Harriet's lovers, and the latter as the known offspring of his elder brother Lord Egremont.[9] But this would do no more than make Caroline and William first cousins, a common relationship between aristocratic brides and grooms at the time without any damaging consequences.

These theories, which come long after the lifetime of the unfortunate Augustus Lamb, do not affect the practical circumstances of his upbringing: the problem that Caroline – and William – had in caring for a son whom convention suggested should be taken from their care; and this was something that neither of them wanted, emotionally in the case of Caroline, guardedly in the case of William Lamb.

Beyond caring for Augustus and pining for Byron, Caroline Lamb now resumed the London life from which she had been torn away at the end of the previous summer. Her 'effigy', to use Lord Byron's word, that is her reputation, was somewhat tarnished by the scandal of the previous year. This did not however lead to any noticeable diminution in her spirit. Her grandmother, for example, commented in February that Caroline was 'better and happier' since her return.[10] Lady Spencer remained a genial presence in her granddaughter's life, which made her death in 1814 – at the age of seventy-seven, a great age for the times – all the sadder.

Returning to Byron's private life, this was in fact more complicated at this point than was publicly apparent. In the spring he was reunited with his beloved half-sister Augusta. Five years older than Byron, after the death of her mother she had been brought up by her maternal grandmother without knowing her half-brother and had begun corresponding with Byron after a few meetings when the latter was at Harrow. As a young woman she looked not unlike Caroline Lamb, with her soulful eyes and neat pointed chin, if not quite so elfinly pretty. Augusta had married her first cousin Colonel George Leigh in 1807: not a happy union given that he was a gambler who ended by leaving his wife and numerous children nothing but debts.

Byron on the other hand was enchanted by Augusta. Amiable easy-going, an outwardly straightforward connection with Byron – what was there not to like?[11] During the summer of 1813 she acted as his frequent companion. And it seems that he confessed his feelings to his favourite confidante – Lady Melbourne. Whatever those feelings might be: there were some dubious phrases in his letters to Lady Melbourne which might indicate that his relationship with Augusta had gone beyond mere emotion, in short that the (half-) brother and sister had committed incest.

To Augusta in turn he confessed that he had been in a 'serious scrape' – an ungallant reference to Caroline – but was now out of it.

At this point there was no reason for Caroline to question the nature of Byron's feelings for his half-sister; it was Byron's feelings for *her*, the enduring legacy of 'that moment', the love she was convinced they had shared, which obsessed her. That might change especially if Byron himself was forthcoming on the subject.

The culmination of the obsession was at the beginning of July 1813. Their relationship had begun with a public gathering at which Lady Caroline Lamb chose to disdain Lord Byron. In effect it ended at another public gathering at which Lord Byron disdained Lady Caroline Lamb. This serves as a reminder of how much of the Byron–Caroline Lamb relationship was played out in public – to the professed indignation of Byron, and with a mixture of pride and despair on the part of Caroline.

It was a summer season of Society balls. There was for example the ball given by Sarah Countess of Jersey, the prodigious heiress to her grandfather Robert Child's vast banking fortune: she was the Chairman of Almack's Club on whose stern nod admission to Society depended. Her character however was the reverse of austere: she was nicknamed Silence, a crude reference to her habit of endless chat. The daughter-in-law of Frances Lady Jersey, powerful mistress of the Prince Regent, Sarah Lady Jersey's personal life was equally colourful: when Lord Jersey was asked why he had never fought a duel to protect her honour, it was said that he replied: Why, that would require him to challenge every man in London.[12]

Fortunately Lady Caroline Lamb had family connections to establish her safely in Lady Jersey's – and Almack's – orbit, even if her 'effigy' was tarnished in the opinion of Lord Byron. That is to say, Lady Jersey's sister Maria was married to Caroline's brother John Lord Duncannon. For a moment it seemed that Caroline would settle comfortably back into the easy conventional social life to which she had been born. At Lady Jersey's Ball, Lord Byron took care not to encounter her. This distressed

Caroline – loyal William dried her tears – but was undoubtedly the diplomatic solution. The Byron imbroglio should be forgotten. Such things happened – and had indeed happened to most of her close relations, if not quite such a flamboyant manifestation.

The ball given by Lady Heathcote in July 1813 put an end to that illusion. Both Byron and Lady Caroline were present: in their different ways figures of twisted glamour, whether the pale, handsome man with his club foot, or the enchanting sprite with her equivalent of a club foot in a reputation for outrages in public. Caroline Lamb gave her own dramatic account of it many years later to Byron's friend Thomas Medwin. It was Caroline whom Lady Heathcote invited to begin the dancing – with the fashionable waltz. Caroline gazed at the silent Byron. 'I conclude I may waltz *now*.' Byron was up to the challenge. She was certainly well able to partner brilliantly 'every body in turn'.[13]

Unfortunately that barbed exchange was not enough for Caroline (though quite enough for Byron). Words gave way to confusion and then something more horrible, the shedding of blood. According to that prejudiced source Lady Melbourne, Frederick Lamb, William's brother, now tried to calm down the increasingly hysterical Caroline. Whereupon she broke a glass deliberately and scratched herself. It seemed that this was not enough: Caroline now picked up a pair of scissors and did some more cutting, although with not much conviction. It was enough however for blood to be shed, and as a result the story reached the press. *The Satirist* of course found the name of Lamb irresistible; writing of Caroline's intention:

> With horn-handled knife
> To kill a tender lamb as dead as mutton[14]

But as it happens, no one was killed, not even one of the many Lambs who were present, and no single person much damaged.

What was ended was any suggestion on either side that Byron and Caroline could have a civilised relationship, a sentimental friendship perhaps in which poetry played its part, or a playful platonic intrigue as it appeared Byron enjoyed with Lady

Melbourne. Caroline continued to make sudden appearances in Byron's life, darting out of nowhere, probably dressed as a page; giving the impression that she loved the daring behaviour nearly as much as she loved Byron himself.

As Byron exclaimed wearily to Lady Melbourne in a letter about one of these 'inroads', as he called them, into Albany: 'she comes at all times, at any time, and the moment the door is open, in she walks. I can't throw her out of the window . . . but I will not receive her.' (Fortunately perhaps for both parties Byron was actually out on this occasion.) After Byron's death a faded invitation to the party was discovered among his papers. On it Byron had scribbled a note which seemed to sum up his attitude: 'This card I keep as a curiosity, for it was at this ball that Lady C.L. performed ye dagger scene – of indifferent memory.'[15]

So Byron did not forget, as his own bitter effusion on the waters of Lethe had already made clear. But he did not intend such scenes should be repeated. He was already feeling a growing desire to leave England. When Lord and Lady Oxford did depart to go travelling, he was even tempted to go with them – was it the lure of little Charlotte or Lady Oxford, lovely in the autumn of her beauty? Here was another prod – a violently public prod – of encouragement.

Colourful reminders of their association remained to irritate, titivate or excite Byron and Caroline. Thomas Phillips was a rising portrait painter of wide-ranging tastes, who had painted the Prince of Wales one year and the next year the great artist and poet William Blake. In 1812 he had begun a picture of Caroline Lamb dressed as a page, short, ruffled hair and all, holding out a platter of fruit. Watching her was a spaniel. There was a double reference – to Jacques Cazotte's Le diable amoureux (1772), where a young man was seduced by 'an enamoured spirit' appearing with a platter of fruit and a spaniel, and to Marlowe's Faust, where the devil took the form of a spaniel.[16]

The picture was actually commissioned by Caroline's ever-loving young cousin Hart, now 6th Duke of Devonshire, who paid forty guineas for it on 2 May 1814 (roughly £5,000 in today's values). Caroline could not help meditating on how suitable the subject matter of the picture would be for John Murray – no doubt bearing in mind that he was Byron's publisher: 'Lamb as a Page, can anything be more appropriate to remind you of me?' It was after all her favourite pose. She ended by giving him a miniature based on the portrait.

The picture itself had temporarily a rather more public fate when Phillips chose to exhibit it in his studio next door to a picture of Lord Byron in robes, which could be mistaken for those of a friar.* Some visitors were fooled into thinking the two pictures were in fact one. Phillips increased the naughty pleasure of the others by deliberately blocking the eyeline of 'Lady Caroline Lamb' – so that she could not catch sight of the wicked 'Lord Byron'.[17]

1814 was a particularly icy winter. There were further overtures from Caroline to Byron in the form of letters, as Byron would describe to his friend Thomas Medwin later. But Caroline was basically at Brocket Hall with Augustus, enjoying that tempestuous riding in the park which assuaged her spirits – until on one particularly chilling day in January she had a bad fall on the ice, which temporarily halted her.

As for Caroline's relationship with her husband, that varied according to the current influence of his family. When Lady Melbourne and William's sister Emily were in the ascendant, both of these strong, intelligent women were determined to rid their beloved brother of his encumbrance of a wife; beyond being strong and intelligent, they were also ambitious, and could not envisage that unreliable fairy sprite as the wife of a successful politician. Marital justice should surely have condemned Caroline Lamb to withdraw altogether from the side of the man she had so flagrantly betrayed. On the other hand, the continued affection which undeniably existed between the couple was obviously a consolation to Harriet Bessborough.

---

* The famous picture of Caroline still hangs at Chatsworth, as Hart had wished. The miniature is still at the offices of John Murray, 50 Albemarle Street, as Caroline had wished.

The hopes of the Lamb family centred on a proper legal Separation between the husband and wife. For this was a time before the introduction of effective divorce laws: divorce was an ecclesiastical matter and almost impossible to secure. A legal Separation was thus the best solution, whereby Caroline would be officially distanced and as a result her actions would no longer reflect on William in the harsh public gaze. In the autumn of 1814, as rumours flew about on the subject, it seemed that this Separation would finally be brought about. Lord Auckland, for example, reported that the actual terms had been worked out.[18]

During this time, following her return from Ireland, Caroline had begun to write. She did not advertise the fact; after all writing, whether sweet poetry or delightful prose, was a perfectly respectable activity for a young lady at the time, like painting or embroidering. Wasn't it? She had always enjoyed the company of writers and literary people: she had indeed genuinely admired Byron's poetry before she met him, and in advance the beauty of his lines contributed as much as the glamour of his personality to her desire for the encounter.

Among her close literary friends was Sydney Lady Morgan. It was in 1811 that Caroline had first encountered the Irish novelist who made her name in 1806 with her novel *The Wild Irish Girl*, at once romantic and liberal. In the words of Lady Morgan's memoirs, Caroline won her 'enduring friendship' and they began a correspondence which did indeed prove lifelong. Sydney Morgan's reactions to her precious friend were in marked contrast to those of many around her. Sydney Morgan was affectionate and she was charitable; she could see what a remarkable person the fairy sprite was without blinding herself to her manifest weaknesses, summed up as follows: 'she was bold and daring in her excursions through the debateable land which divides the territories of friendship from those of love. If she never fell, she was scarcely ever safe from falling.' From the first Sydney Morgan had remarked that 'the exercise of her pencil and pen' were among the ways in which Caroline Lamb satisfied her eternal craving after excitement.[19]

Another female celebrity at the time was Madame Germaine de Staël, daughter of Louis XVI's finance minister, Jacques Necker. Having enjoyed great success as a voice of moderation during the Revolution, she took refuge in England. Here Madame de Staël's study *De L'Allemagne*, banned in France, was published by John Murray, and she joined his circle; other works were published by Henry Colburn. Caroline Lamb enjoyed the honour of the company of such a talented woman: perhaps it did Madame de Staël no harm in her eyes that this literary lady in her late forties failed to exert her charms over Lord Byron.

At the beginning of 1814, the poet reported to Lady Melbourne in the course of one of his disloyal grumbles about Lady Caroline: 'Her [Madame de Staël's] books are very delightful – but in society I see nothing but a very plain woman forcing one to listen and look at her with her pen behind her ear and her mouth full of *ink* [sic].' He then rambled on about other women as he was accustomed to do to his confidante, before resuming with a reassuringly condescending dismissal of Lady Melbourne's daughter-in-law: 'C [sic] may do as she pleases – thanks to your good nature rather than my merits or prudence – there is little to dread from her love – and I forgive her hatred.'[20]

Then things in Europe took a better turn – from the point of view of the English – with what was believed to be the final defeat of Napoleon, self-styled Emperor of the French, in April 1814; he was exiled to the isle of Elba off the coast of Tuscany. The release of the continent from Napoleon's thrall would surely lead to the happy resumption of visiting on the part of the aristocratic classes.

Together William and Caroline went to a masked ball at Watier's Club on 1 July, in honour of Napoleon's defeat. Seventeen hundred people were said to have been there, all dressed in masks and dominoes. Among them was Lord Byron, persuaded to attend by his friend John Hobhouse. In the course of the evening Caroline and Byron had a long conversation and he did not leave until morning. Perhaps to Caroline it seemed that nothing could keep them apart.

Byron however appears to have been spurred on by the meeting to ask Lady Melbourne for help to renew his suit to Annabella Milbanke, having assured her that he had done all he could to end the relationship with Caroline. The gap between their respective attitudes to their shared past was growing: the dagger (or was it a glass?) at the Heathcote Ball had not shed much blood in actual fact, but there was a possibility that it had severed something intangible, Byron's thread of love for Caroline Lamb.

It was perhaps just as well for Caroline that a new, very different relationship was just beginning to be developed, even though there was once more a connection to Byron. It also appealed to that other – never to be forgotten – intelligent side of Caroline Lamb. Isaac Nathan was the man in question.

Isaac Nathan was a Jewish musician and composer, now aged twenty-four (four years younger than Caroline), whose parents had been refugees from Poland. His portrait shows a strong, handsome face with heavily marked eyebrows above large dark eyes and a long, straight nose. He was brought up in Canterbury, of which it was said: 'The Jews of this city [about thirty families] are not numerous but they are highly respectable'; Nathan's father was a Cantor and the boy had consequently been nurtured on rabbinical teachings as well as the rich history and mythology of Hebrew tradition. At a time when the measures against Jews were being slowly relaxed, he attended the first Jewish boarding school in Cambridge and after that managed to go to the University (although Jews could not take degrees). After Cambridge it was intended that he should follow in his father's footsteps. Music however was his passion.[21]

Nathan was therefore apprenticed to Domenico Corri, a Neapolitan musician and singing-master. It was a successful start: he himself became both a composer and teacher, with his first London concert in 1813. He married his seventeen-year-old pupil, Elizabeth Rosetta Worthington, a gentile; it was notable that, rarely for her time, she proceeded to convert to Judaism.

Lady Caroline Lamb's association with Isaac Nathan began in 1814 when she wrote a poem to celebrate the future marriage of her younger brother Willy Ponsonby to Lady Barbara Ashley

Cooper, daughter of the Earl of Shaftesbury. Isaac Nathan set it to music as a duet and it was sung at the engagement party. Thereafter he set ten of her songs to music, and when they were published Caroline generously allowed him the copyright. The pair performed the song together: Nathan with his fine tenor voice, and Caroline with her love of both harp and harpsichord.[22]

Nathan was ambitious. His intention, in view of the current success of Tom Moore's *Irish Melodies*, was to do something similar with Hebrew melodies – but he needed the poems for the melodies. His first thought was Sir Walter Scott, but on being turned down he went for Byron, who was enjoying great commercial success at the time. Byron's recent poem *The Corsair*, published by John Murray, caused the latter to exclaim: 'I believe I have sold 13,000 copies, a thing unprecedented.'[23]

Nathan wrote a long letter to Lord Byron which began with an apology for 'the unwarrantable liberty' in addressing him and then went on to plead his case. He would set the poems to music. He praised Byron's work *The Bride of Abydos* before continuing: 'I have since been persuaded by several Ladies of known fame and literary genius [inclination], to apply to your Lordship, even at the risk of seeming impertinence on my part . . .'.[24] It seems likely that Caroline encouraged him to add this phrase – which certainly did not underestimate her place in Society. Whether Byron recognised the allusion to Caroline or not, the appeal worked, with the independent support of Byron's friend Douglas Kinnaird.

Lord Byron now began a close association with Isaac Nathan as he worked on what would become his *Hebrew Melodies*, published in 1815. It was dedicated to the young Princess Charlotte, daughter of the Prince Regent, to whom Nathan had taught music. Among them was the incomparable love poem beginning,

She walks in beauty, like the night
Of cloudless climes and starry skies;
And all that's best of dark and bright
Meet in her aspect and her eyes . . .

Which became (and remains) an exquisite song at Isaac Nathan's hands. The *Melodies*, published in a large folio costing one guinea, were a prodigious success. Ten thousand copies of this and a second edition were sold.[25] Byron himself frequently requested to hear 'She Walks in Beauty' sung and would not infrequently join in: he judged 'a melancholy expression' to be appropriate on these occasions.

The intimacy of poet and musician can be judged by Nathan's decision to send Byron 'some holy biscuits, commonly called unleavened bread' – in other words *matzos* – so that 'a certain angel at a certain hour' would guide him on his travels. Byron responded gratefully: 'the unleavened bread shall certainly accompany me in my pilgrimage: the Motzas [*sic*] shall be to me a charm against the destroying angel . . .'.

Meanwhile Caroline Lamb enjoyed Nathan's friendship, with its subtext of love poems set to music. While she still dreamt of Byron, she was beginning to experience something very different. This was the insidious excitement which creativity brings, and along with excitement a special kind of joy, whatever the consequences of the creation.

As for these consequences, it was possible of course for a pen to be used as a metaphorical dagger, as well as a romantic painter's brush. A pretty woman as well as a plain woman like Madame de Staël could have ink flowing in her veins. Would Lady Caroline Lamb now wield her pen as she had once brandished her dagger? If so, the scene might be not so easily dismissed by Lord Byron.

PART THREE

========

EVERYONE KNOWS
WHO WROTE
THE BOOK

*'I have . . . written a most beautiful preface – & now wish to have
done with the whole thing – it is useless to deny it – everyone knows
who wrote the Book – make therefore what use you choose of it . . .'*

Lady Caroline Lamb to Henry Colburn, 1816

CHAPTER SEVEN

============

Active in Paris

'Nothing is agissant *but Caroline William*
in a purple riding habit.'

Harriet Granville, Paris 1815

T HE AUTUMN OF 1814 was marked by a renewal of Lord
Byron's suit to Annabella Milbanke – this time with success. They
became engaged and, somewhat to the surprise of the world,
Caroline managed to write a polite note of congratulation. They
were married on 2 January 1815, although their correspondence beforehand appears marked with uncertainty. Less than a
fortnight earlier Annabella had added a postscript to a letter:
'Are you less confident than you were in the happiness of our
marriage?' To which Byron's answer was something less than
encouraging: 'I do not see any good purpose to which questions
of this kind are to lead – nor can they be answered otherwise
than by time and events.'[1]

Shortly after this particular event, Lady Melbourne carried out
her duty as she saw it and took Caroline with her to visit the
newly married Byrons, then at Piccadilly Terrace. Whatever had
been feared from the little volcano of yesteryear, Caroline sat
in subdued silence. She described the occasion later to Thomas
Medwin. It was 'a cruel request', Caroline said, adding that 'it

had actually been made by Byron'. Present were Augusta Leigh, Lady Melbourne, Annabella Byron, Lady Noel (as Annabella's mother was now designated for reasons of inheritance) and Caroline herself: five women who, with the exception of Lady Noel, could all argue that they enjoyed or had enjoyed a special intimacy with the poet. (Although she did not need to point that out to Medwin.) Byron, she said, appeared agitated: 'his hand was cold but he seemed kind'.[2]

Correspondence, an altogether lighter experience, continued. There was a teasing letter to Byron a little later beginning: 'My Lord, Altho' you have got a lovely new Wife – an Elegant new Carriage – and a Beautiful new Seal . . .'. Caroline then pointed out that there were others who might not have wives but still had seals 'as well as you'. And she quoted *Crede Biron*, an evident allusion to that bonfire and the footmen with their mocking '*Ne crede Biron*' buttons.[3]

But in general Caroline's conduct was calm, which came as a blessed relief to her relations – and no doubt to Byron as well. It was the pen, that pen which might eventually turn into a dagger, which was beginning to provide her with a deceptive tranquillity – deceptive in the sense that one day the outside world might not perceive its effects as quite so tranquil.

The obsession had been slowly growing. Two years ago, with typical self-mockery, Caroline had described to Lady Holland at some length her unsatisfactory attempts at being an author. She had looked at her novel, which Lady Holland had been good enough to say she would read, all scribbled nine volumes of it; and by erasing 'all that was bad & all that was dull' had reduced it to three pages. 'One of these', continued Caroline, 'was borrowed from an old Author, one was beautiful, but Dearest Lady Holland: I am now writing a Comedy & you are one of the Dramatis Personae. We get up at 8 literally & go to bed at 11 & sleep.' This ideal life was rounded off with a postscript: 'Wm is very well & we are very comfortable – Augustus looks radiant & is growing tender hearted – he is Wm's delight and never far from him. He looks really beautiful in his new dress – which is plain & not as I daresay you think all over gold & silver.'[4] (Lady Holland was evidently inclined to tease Caroline over her indulgent love for her son.)

If the ideal life was short-lived, on this and other occasions, it is clear that somewhere in Caroline's imagination lurked the inspiring picture of herself at work on a novel, with William and Augustus, her intimate family, near at hand – and happy.

In the meantime, in the world around them time and events were producing dramatic results in the development of the Napoleonic Wars. From the point of view of the Bessborough family, for example, the summer of 1815 was the best of times, the worst of times, in a phrase which Dickens would immortalise forty years later. After ten months of exile Napoleon escaped from Elba in late February 1815; three weeks later the diarist Charles Greville gloomily reported: 'The Success of Bonaparte is considered certain . . .'. The prophets were wrong. At Waterloo on 18 June the Duke of Wellington, with the aid of Marshal Blücher, finally defeated the seemingly invincible Napoleon. He wrote to one of his lady friends to reassure her about his own personal safety: 'The finger of Providence was upon me and I escaped unhurt.'[5]

Harriet Bessborough broke the news to Maria Duncannon, her daughter-in-law, with an understandable allusion to Napoleon's earlier escape: 'We have this moment heard of B[onaparte's] surrender. What an astonishing history it has been, but will he not be a puzzling person to take care of?'[6]

Unfortunately the finger of Providence had not been upon one of the Bessboroughs' sons, Frederick Ponsonby. Caroline reported to the publisher John Murray: 'I am very miserable, they have just ordered my brave Brother & his Regiment the 12th [Dragoons] to Flanders.' She was right to feel fear on his behalf. As Greville now reported: 'The news of this victory was received in England with a general joy which was considerably dampened by the magnitude of the loss sustained.'[7]

Fred, who had joined the army at sixteen, fought in the Peninsular War and was wounded at Salamanca, which he brushed off as 'a little accident' in a letter home. Now he fought gallantly at Waterloo, but suffered a far more horrific fate: he fell off his horse in the midst of a charge. When he tried to get up, a French lancer spotted him and with the furious words, '*Coquin, tu n'est pas mort* [rascal, you are not dead],' plunged in his weapon. Fred, by now both stabbed and shot, simply lay there as he was 'rode over by the Prussian cavalry', with the most appalling bruises on his whole body as a result.[8] As Fred himself wrote about this equine assault, with remarkable tolerance: 'I was a good deal hurt by the horses, in general horses will avoid treading upon men but the Field was so covered they had no space for their feet.' So he stayed, for eighteen hours, a blood-stained body given for dead, while callous observers swarmed over the field and robbed him. Miraculously, Fred struggled back to life. A glass of brandy given by a compassionate French officer probably saved his life.*

Caroline and William together rushed to Brussels and were the first of the family to arrive on 6 July. Harriet Bessborough, who was in Italy, came racing across the continent to join them. Significantly, Caroline dropped a quick line to John Murray just before she left referring to a manuscript and drawings which he was to receive – 'I am just setting out for Brussels & shall be obliged to you to write to me constantly there as I will to you – I must to the post office.'[10]

The next day Caroline wrote to her brother John Duncannon: 'I have just seen Frederick, & thank God he is said to be out of danger . . . How happy I feel at having come. Poor Fred wants the greatest care & attention.' Fortunately he was looked after by the surgeon who attended the Prince of Orange. 'I am to see him tomorrow at 12. I scarce can write, I feel so very nervous but happy. Only his breath seems very affected, but the surgeon says he is doing well.' Touchingly for Caroline, Fred asked after Augustus before all the other family members and 'particularly wished' Caroline to have brought him with her: not a very practical thought but one which filled the mother with joy.[11]

---

* Frederick Ponsonby subsequently became a Major-General and Governor of Malta. While he was there, in casual conversation with a Frenchman about the Battle of Waterloo, he discovered he was talking to his saviour.[9]

To Lady Melbourne Caroline gave a rather different report. It was a grisly account of 'the great amusement at Brussels, indeed the only one except visiting the sick'. This was to 'make large parties & go to the field of Battle – & pick up a skull or a grape shot or an old shoe or a letter & bring it home'. She added that William had paid the visit but she would not go unless Fred got better and wanted her to go with him.

Where visiting the sick was concerned, there was conviviality of course, lightly wounded officers reclining with pretty ladies visiting them. But in the main: 'it is rather heart breaking to be here . . . & one goes blubbering about – seeing such fine people without their legs & arms – some in agony'.

Caroline ended by noting how the Duchess of Richmond's 'fatal' Ball on the eve of Waterloo was still coming in for censure: 'there never was such a Ball – so fine & so sad – all the young Men who appeared there shot dead – a few hours after . . .'.[12]

Since the Bessboroughs had joined Caroline and William in Brussels, it was his parents who took Fred home in August 1815. This left the Lambs free to travel on to Paris, where they were happy to think that they would find Hart, the Duke of Devonshire, Caroline's childhood friend and admirer; although the bachelor Hart was by this time enjoying an equally doomed *amitié amoureuse* with the Prince Regent's daughter Princess Charlotte. They would also find the victor of Waterloo himself. The great Duke had crossed the border shortly after the battle, to the music of regimental bands playing 'The girl I left behind me'. Napoleon had abdicated in favour of his son, the four-year-old King of Rome, currently in Vienna with his mother the Austrian-born Empress Marie Louise; the way was becoming clear for the restoration of Louis XVIII as the representative of the Bourbon monarchy.

By the time William and Caroline reached Paris, Napoleon was heading for exile on a distant island in the South Atlantic, while Wellington was installed in triumph. The great Germaine de Staël, for example, hailed him as a god: 'My Lord! There is a glory in this world which is unalloyed and without reproach . . . As you wake up in the morning does not your heart beat with the joy of being you?' Fanny Burney, the novelist, married to a member of Louis XVIII's bodyguard, was similarly ecstatic: 'Immortal Wellington! *Vive! Vive! Vive!*'. Everlastingly a focus for the ladies, everlastingly contented with that position, on a somewhat lower level than that of a deity the Duke had already been the subject of enjoyable gossip before the battle when he was said to have flirted with the pretty young Lady Frances Wedderburn-Webster at the Duchess of Richmond's Ball. The relationship, whether consummated or not, became complicated by the possibility of lawsuits, first of all by her husband for adultery, and then by both Websters against the press for alleging that adultery. One item in both the English and European press was headed 'Fashionable Alliteration'; it asserted:

> In the letter W. there's a charm half divine
> War-Wellington-Wedderburn-Webster – and Wine.[13]

It did not take very long before Lady Caroline Lamb reached her own decision about the charm of the letter W.

When it came to enjoyment of life, there was no doubt that it was more fun to set her cap, as it were, at the letter W in Paris than remain plunged in melancholy at the thought of the letter B, married and in England. A sporadic correspondence with Lord Byron continued to take place, but in the meantime there was the whole Parisian scene in the aftermath of war, beginning with the amazing sight of the Champs-Elysées thronging with British troops. Paris rejoiced in its freedom: fashions, for example, became extreme. The high-waisted Empire dresses were now bell-shaped with masses of feminine flounces round the hem – what Hart called 'immense bouffées'.[14]

One extraordinary night at the opera was described by Caroline's cousin Harryo who was present in Paris with her diplomat husband (Lady Bessborough's former lover), recently created Viscount Granville: 'The House was full and brilliant beyond measure and my brother [Hart] in raptures . . . All Nations, all Embassies, all English men . . . But what do you think they shout at and applaud . . . They dance the Battle of Waterloo in all its details. The Imperial Guard wounded, form dejected groups, embrace the National Guard etc. whilst a smart English officer makes most brilliant Entrees. He is Hèros de la Pièce ... The French all kneel to him and kiss the Hem of his garment and dance a Finale of all the Nations amidst bursts of applause.' This astonishing celebration by the French of what had been a colossal defeat was witnessed among others by Metternich in the box of Lady Castlereagh.[15]

In Paris Harryo continued to offer those wry comments on her cousin's progress that she had been making in effect since their shared childhood; she gave a typically amusing report to her sister Georgiana Morpeth on 1 September: 'Nothing is *agissant* [active] but Caroline William in a purple riding habit, tormenting everybody' – no bonnet and waistless dress for Caroline. Harriet went on: 'but I am convinced already primed for an attack upon the Duke of Wellington, and I have no doubt that she will to a certain extent succeed, as no dose of flattery is too strong for him to swallow or her to administer'. After a further account of Caroline's journey to Paris, punctuated by visits to French apothecaries along the way, Harryo ended on a joke: 'on arrival, Caroline sent immediately for a doctor, but by mistake they went for the Duke of Wellington'.[16]

Certainly Caroline Lamb was out to enjoy her time in Paris, after the horrifying anxiety regarding her brother. There was a story of a party at which the great Prussian Marshal Blücher was expected. But did not arrive. And did not arrive. Then distant hurrahs were heard, growing louder. In strode Caroline in a cocked hat and a greatcoat! Having enjoyed her laugh and her triumph, Caroline wheedled up to Lord Hardwicke for the greatest favour – money – to pay the servants for their pretty hurrahs, 'and they did it so beautifully'. Triumphant, she ran away delighted to deliver the reward to the servants. The whole story was typical of the young woman Wellington would get to know: the fun, the bravado – and the thoughtfulness for her helpers.

The Duke, Germaine de Staël's god, was at this point a man in his mid-forties, an upstanding manly figure, as is attested by his portraits of the time. His marriage to Kitty Pakenham had not been a success: it was in fact a sad marriage, sad in the sense that they both would have been happier married to different people. Wellington, as has been noted, responded in traditional male fashion by flirtations, to use an encompassing word; but he also particularly enjoyed female friendship, and as the years passed his friendship with Mrs Harriet Arbuthnot would become one of the important aspects of his private life.

What Lady Caroline Lamb was able to offer to the great man was something else again: amusement. Her cousin Harryo Gran-ville admitted ruefully: 'I see she amuses him [Wellington] to the greatest degree, especially her accidents which is the charitable term he gives to all her sorties.' There were aspects of friendship and flirtation as well in the amusement, of course; but there was a further element which would develop as time went on. Caroline aroused in the Duke of Wellington protective feelings, the same feelings, it has been suggested by one of Wellington's biographers, as were later aroused by Sarah Countess of Jersey, for being 'someone whose tongue ran away with her and got her into trouble'.[17] Perhaps they were to a small degree something of the same feelings, the tenderness, which preserved Caroline's marriage to William, to the baffled fury of the women in his family.

And for once the Byron connection was seen in a completely different light: not as lending her glamour (as would happen increasingly in the eyes of the young as the years went by) but as being responsible for the disasters in her life. Wellington the man of action, in short, had a distaste for Byron, one of 'your professional poets' who 'praise fine sentiments and never practise them'. Later he would refer to this distaste to Lady Shelley, based on the fact that Byron had been 'the ruining of her [Caroline's] life'.[18]

In Paris, Caroline might amuse the great Duke, but she did not altogether desert those habits of self-advertisement for which she was famous – or, to use the favourite word of her detractors, infamous. There was the notorious scene of the busted bust. Caroline Hamilton, sister of the Duchess of Wellington, was present at the dinner party, which included Marshal Blücher, and described the incident. A plaster-of-Paris bust of the great Duke by a young French artist had been placed on the dining-room table to be assessed. Thinking it a rotten likeness, Caroline Lamb picked the bust up and hurled it to the ground, smashing it into pieces.

There was a shudder from Society. For once William Lamb shared the distaste. He said to himself – but loud enough for his neighbour, Wellington's sister-in-law Caroline Hamilton, to hear the words: 'Very foolish indeed!' She turned to him and said coldly: 'Indeed I think so.'[19]

Caroline Lamb's dalliance with Michael Bruce was a very different matter. Here was no profound contrast to her recent melancholy involvement, but something that was on the contrary uncomfortably nostalgic. Bruce has in fact been described as 'a wealthy adventurer in the Byronic mould' – except of course he was far from being a great poet.[20]

There was another comparison to Byron in Wellington's low opinion of both men. Bruce was one of three young Englishmen who organised the escape of Napoleon's supporter, the Comte de Lavalette, husband of the Empress Josephine's niece Émilie de Beauharnais. Condemned to death like Marshal Ney, after the latter's execution Lavalette managed with their help to escape disguised in his wife's clothes. Then, with forged passports and further disguises, Lavalette made his way first to England and finally back to Bavaria, where he was able to take advantage of his Beauharnais connection. All this disgusted Wellington. Now known as 'Lavalette' Bruce, the young Englishman in Wellington's opinion deserved to be hanged. Wellington made his view, which was probably tinged with a certain jealousy, clear to Caroline Lamb; although to do him justice Wellington then used his influence to see that the three men, including Bruce, got minimum prison sentences.[21]

Caroline's involvement with Bruce preceded this dramatic episode. It was very far from being the first romantic encounter Bruce had had with an English aristocratic lady of note. As a young man (he was born in 1787, two years after Caroline) he had left Cambridge without a degree to go travelling; and for three years had been the lover and travelling companion of Lady Hester Stanhope, first encountered in Malta. He thus displayed a taste for women's wit (once denounced by Byron himself as 'that dangerous thing') which would have pleased the sparkling Caroline. During these journeys he actually met Byron himself, in 1810, the period recorded in *Childe Harold*. All of this was grist to the romantic mill of Lady Caroline Lamb. She delighted in addressing Bruce in correspondence as 'Star of the East' and 'He of the Desert'.[22]

There was further fun to be had from the fact that her mother-in-law once again was thought to fancy Bruce. Caroline Lamb's sister-in-law, the former Caroline St Jules, now wife of George Lamb, reported with disgust: 'to crown all my gossip and scandal there is my belle mère tres serieusement amoureuse de Monsr Bruce who is neither handsome nor pleasant, but very conceited and I am doomed to hear her's and Caro's mutual confidences of how the other makes up to him'. Never mind that Caroline William assured her that she, Caroline George, was the true object of Bruce's affection: 'but I am not taken in so he comforts himself with her'. Caroline George added coldly: 'This family is enough to make one sick.'[23]

Lady Caroline's relationship with Bruce is probably best compared with her earliest public flirtation with Sir Godfrey Webster; except that the world she was (or was not) outraging was that of post-war Paris, not Whig High Society. The growth of her friendship with the great Duke of Wellington was of far greater importance to her, as time passed. The two men themselves, Byron and Bruce, had much in common: handsome and dissipated, with awesome reputations for female conquest. It has been noted that Caroline later assured Lord Byron that this earlier Webster relationship had been dalliance, not a full-blown love affair. It is frankly unlikely that the affair with Michael Bruce fell into the same category of dalliance. Writing to Bruce later in a reminiscent and partly regretful mood, Caroline chose the romantic words 'errors of the wandering heart' – a phrase which left open the question of the wandering body . . . The fact that Caroline was now the former lover of Byron rather than a spotless young married woman as she had been in Webster's day suggests that, however briefly, they were actual lovers. At the same time, what Caroline enjoyed about her relationship with Bruce was once again, as with Webster, the professions of desire and the general to-do. But she was having fun rather than expressing the desperate passion she had felt for Byron.

A poem written to Bruce was illustrated by Caroline herself with a sketch of two charming little figures, one apparently lifeless, the other a pretty Cupid inserting an arrow in her breast:

> Love seiz'd for her his sweetest dart
> And plunged it in her guilty heart
> Even when entwined within his arms
> She gazed upon his matchless charms
> Even as she pressed his lips of rose
> And heard the music of his vows
> The subtle poison through her frame
> Burst like the wild insatiate flame.
> Remorse, despair and agony
> Mingled with every extasy
> One kiss, one last forced kiss he tried
> She gave him what he wished – and died.[24]

Her last letter before the Melbourne party left Paris strikes an affectionate, regretful note rather than thwarted passion, as does the suggestion that he should bring others to his farewell visit: 'Star of the East I go tomorrow & must entreat you to call on me tonight till one. You will find me at Home. Pray bring the inconstant [Benjamin Constant, the political philosopher, once the lover of Madame de Staël] and any other you may find – how I regret the Bruce on quitting Paris – aye and all else in this delightful capital. Yours with respect & truth Caroline.'[25]

It seems most likely then that Michael Bruce was the first of Caroline's clever, amusing, intelligent admirers, enriching her life with their professed devotion (while not risking very much by that profession). This might be the way she would go in the future, as being finally more satisfactory than the consequences of real-life 'Remorse, despair and agony/Mingled with every extasy' experienced with Byron.

There is another aspect to Caroline's 'affair' with Michael Bruce which is also an augury for the future. William Lamb evidently continued to have excellent polite social relations with him. One letter from Caroline to Bruce while still in Paris is focused on William's desire 'to join your party', despite Caroline having 'a small attack of fever'.[26] As a result of the visit to fashionable post-war Paris, a new detachment in William's attitude to Caroline was emerging. It was the beginning of an indifference to Caroline *agissant*, which might or might not result in true alienation. Whatever he had suffered in the past, it is clear that William did not really suffer now – not however for lack of tenderness: his protective kindness remained.

The Lambs returned to England from Paris in October. Caroline's mind was now focused on something rapidly becoming of prime importance to her: creativity in place of sexuality. She returned not only to England, but to that piece of writing with which she had been half toying, half pursuing, for several years. Caroline *agissant* was looking to find a more serious occupation to replace that passion in all its ecstatic and grim aspects, the thrilling lyre to whose music she had responded. There were many other kinds of passion that she, Caroline Lamb, might evoke, as she was about to discover.

CHAPTER EIGHT

Passion

'It was one of those faces which, having once beheld, we never afterwards forget. It seemed as if the soul of passion had been stamped and printed on every feature.'

Lady Caroline Lamb, *Glenarvon*, 1816

THE NOVEL THAT Lady Caroline Lamb had been writing intermittently for some years would be called *Glenarvon* on publication. But first there was the vital question: who would actually publish it?

Naturally Caroline's first port of call was John Murray: Byron's publisher, Byron's friend, and already tangled with Caroline on many issues to do with the poet, including the episode of the portrait and the forged signature. She had already sent some chapters before the question arose of departing for Brussels. The covering letter struck that touchingly insincere note common to many nervous authors: 'if its execrable in your estimation you can say that it is not so happy as you expected – I shall not be offended'.[1] More chapters followed, and the novel was virtually complete before the Lambs set off to rescue Fred.

The complications began on their return in the autumn – and they were not entirely to do with Caroline's work. Increasingly obsessed by this work in general, she had sent two allegedly anonymous plays, presumably by her, to Annabella Byron, hoping that Byron's connection to a West End theatre might help to get them on. But the Lambs had returned into a Society in which extremely unpleasant rumours of the trouble in Byron's own marriage were rife. Annabella Byron would give birth to a daughter, to be known as Ada, on 10 December 1815: a child that Byron would once feel able to describe as 'sole daughter of my house and heart'. In the tart opinion of Elizabeth Duchess of Devonshire, on the other hand, Ada would soon be described as 'so clever and entertaining' that she hoped she would have none of her father's faults.[2]

In spite of this apparently happy circumstance, the rumours had substance. 'Don't give yourself up to the abominable trade of versifying,' Annabella wrote waspishly on one occasion, hardly appropriate advice for a celebrated poet; she added, which was perhaps the point, 'And brandy.' And the unpleasantness deepened as there was talk of two horrifying unnatural relationships. The first one, involving sodomy, was an actual criminal offence at the time; the second, incest with his sister Augusta, not actually illegal as such but considered equally shocking.

In early January 1816, Annabella Byron left her husband, taking the baby with her. Despite the harsh laws of the time which granted married mothers no rights of custody over their children, Byron as father did not exact his dues at this point and that departure at least was permitted to her.

When Caroline Lamb heard the news, her immediate reaction was to write urgently to John Murray: 'Can you call on me this Evening or tomorrow Morning & do for God sake tell me – have you breathed *what I told you* [italics added] to any one, & if not, have you heard the reports – is it really true & do you know why – they say it is certain – every thing is rumoured as cause of it even the worst possible – I have been literally ill on account of it – pray write.'[3] This letter makes it clear that '*what I told you*' refers to the scandalous or illegal practices with which the world was beginning to charge Byron. And that Caroline, by her own admission, had told at least one person about them. John Murray was likely for his own reasons to keep his mouth shut. Others with their own interests at heart might not be so discreet. And then there was Annabella herself.

At the beginning, to her credit, Caroline actually desired to save the marriage. Her love for Byron – the passion she permitted to rule her life – persuaded her that he should not be allowed to be ruined in the world's eyes. Caroline proceeded to write a series of emotional letters to Byron which suggest that she had at least hinted at his illegal or disreputable behaviour to Annabella herself. Indeed, Caroline's distress at the present time is convincing proof that she had in some way called attention to Byron's homoerotic past as well as his incestuous relationship with his sister Augusta: knowledge she would have gained from Byron himself. She had in fact paid a call on Annabella in March at the house of her sister-in-law Caroline George. It was there she told her things which, if Byron was menaced with them '*the knowledge shall make him tremble*'.

She was prepared to attest now that these allegations were false: 'Lord Byron hear me & for God sake pause before you rashly believe any report others may make – if letter or report or ought else has been malignantly placed in the hands of yr Wife to ruin you I am ready to swear that I did it for the purpose of deceiving her.' She went on: 'there is nothing however base it may appear that I would not do to save you or yours from this – do not oh do not believe those who would lead you for one moment to think she knows anything for certain . . .'.[4]

This heroic stage did not last. As Caroline came to learn more about Byron's treatment of Annabella, she identified herself with this new victim. Switching sides, her vehement letters were now addressed to the wife, not the husband.

'Lady Byron,' she wrote, 'though you are spotless & pure & I am all that is fallen and worthless yet hear me – it is on my knees I write to you . . . for your dear child's sake for your poor Mothers – trust no one – there are serpants [*sic*] round who can smile on you & bite you to the heart . . .'.[5] A well-wisher of the unfortunate Annabella might have pointed out that arguably among these serpents could be counted Lady Caroline Lamb for her revelations about Byron's past. But Caroline's distasteful conduct, as it must fairly be described, was not due to malice as such. It was due to the fact that where Byron or anything to do with Byron was concerned, passion continued to skew her judgement. It was Byron's heart, not Annabella's, which obsessed her.

All this time the separate drama of the novel was being enacted. Caroline did indeed extract every possible dramatic detail from the process. She recounted the following episode with relish to her friend Sydney Morgan. The final manuscript was to be produced for her by a famous 'copier', old Mr Woodcock. Caroline sent him a message to come to Melbourne House. When he arrived he found the governess, Miss Welsh, elegantly dressed, seated at the harp and naturally assumed her to be Lady Caroline Lamb. Miss Welsh pointed to a boy in page's clothes, looking about fourteen. Woodcock could not believe that 'this schoolboy' had written such a thing. The charade continued. When Woodcock returned in a few days, he found Caroline in her proper female identity, informing him that the young author, a certain William Ormond, was dead.[6] Besides the preservation of the author's identity, Caroline was enjoying once again that pleasure which she had discovered long ago, playing the role of a boy-girl page.

John Murray, after hesitating in view of his obvious connection to Byron, finally rejected *Glenarvon*. Caroline then turned to Henry Colburn, a man of roughly her age, already a successful publisher, who had set up in 1806 on the site of Morgan's Circulating Library in Conduit Street and published French and German novels in translation. Notably he produced books by female authors, including Sydney Morgan's *France* the year after *Glenarvon*; and in the same year brought out the first number of the *Literary Gazette*, which was to become the authoritative magazine for the arts and literature. Colburn recognised the potential worth – in money or dynamite – of the novel. He paid Lady Caroline Lamb £200, with a further £300 to come.*

---

* Just under £20,000 and £30,000 in modern values.

Lord Byron
(Thomas Phillips, 1813)

Lady Caroline Lamb,
dressed as a page. It hangs
at Chatsworth (Thomas
Phillips, commissioned by
the Duke of Devonshire).

Lord Byron's chambers, Albany

Annabella Milbanke,
Lady Byron

The Duke of Wellington in his fifties (Sir Thomas Lawrence, 1824)

Brocket Hall in Essex, Caroline's favourite country retreat

John Murray, publisher of Lord Byron

Copies of *Glenarvon*, Caroline's notorious novel
based on Byron, given by her to the Duke of
Wellington. Now in the library at Stratfield Saye,
with the Wellington crest on them.

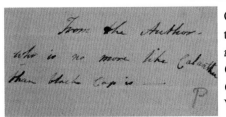

Caroline's dedication of *Glenarvon*
to Wellington: '*From the Author
who is no more Calantha than black
Cap is.*' Calantha is a character in
Glenarvon; black Cap may refer to
Wellington's friend Mrs Arbuthnot.

Caroline's admirer Michael Bruce, an adventurer

Caroline's poem to Michael Bruce beginning: 'Love seiz'd for her his sweetest dart'; her sketch shows Cupid plunging in the dart.
The poem ends:
    'One kiss, one last forced kiss he tried
    She gave him what he wished – and died.'

Love seiz'd for her his sweet dart
And plung'd it in her guilty heart
Even while entranc'd within his arms
she gaz'd upon his matchless charms
Even as she press'd his lips of rose
And heard the music of his vows
The subtle poison through her frame
Burst like the wild insatiate flame.
remorse – dispair and agony
mingl'd with every extacy
one kiss – one last forc'd kiss he tried –
she gave him what he wish'd – and died.

Ugo Foscolo, Italian novelist and Caroline's friend (Francois Xavier Pascal Fabre, 1813)

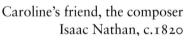

Caroline's friend, the composer Isaac Nathan, c.1820

Bulwer Lytton, Caroline's young admirer, later the celebrated Victorian novelist Lord Lytton (Henry William Pickersgill)

Lady Caroline with her son Augustus, a self-portrait and sketch from her own commonplace book

Letter to Caroline from Augustus Lamb, August 1827, when he was 20. He asks 'My deare Mother' not to send him books to Dublin (where he had accompanied his father as Irish Secretary) since 'Mr Lamb has several books here which I can read.'

Phœnix Park August the 31st 1827

My dear Mother

My Thigh is getting better every day I was very much obliged by your kind letter and many thanks for the enclosed. I am much obliged to you for offering to send me some books but as Mr Lamb has several books here which I can read I think it is not necessary to send any so great a distance. My best love to Susan I hope you are all quite well at Brockett

St Etheldreda's Church, Hatfield, where Lady Caroline Lamb was buried in 1828.

Caroline approached the venture with her usual spirit – and a remarkable confidence in her own spelling. It must be remembered that this was her first book. Evidently some alterations were proposed – or rather made. 'I prefer abiding by my own errors whatever they are than any other persons,' she wrote to Colburn. 'I shall be seriously angry if any alteration is made whatever either in punctuation or orthography and I entreat you to send me the proof sheets.'[7]

One problem concerned Caroline's determination that her songs, set to music by her new friend (and Byron's composer) Isaac Nathan, should be included. When Byron's *Hebrew Melodies* first appeared in 1815, with music by Isaac Nathan, Caroline was in a prickly mood where Byron was concerned since it was shortly after his marriage to Annabella. *Hebrew Melodies* had, as we have seen, been an astonishing success in terms of sales. Caroline on the other hand professed herself disappointed. Claiming that Byron had dashed off the lyrics thoughtlessly, she reflected on 'a childish pride that our poets now cherish to note the number of minutes a day in which they write a thing'. She then picked on 'She Walks in Beauty like the Night' and said she had no doubt the name of Byron would give even these lines grace, but even a song should make sense.[8] This was ridiculous pettiness masking deep sadness at the marriage.

Now Caroline Lamb's genuine passion for music, for playing it herself, especially the harp and the harpsichord, enabled her to relish Nathan's work. Colburn was less sure. He finally bowed to her and included two of her songs – but then chose to omit the music. Caroline wrote to Colburn saying she was 'quite vexed at seeing the songs without the music – will you not add the notes . . . these two are not pretty without music'.[9] In the second edition the notes were printed. A little of this persistence obviously derived from Isaac Nathan's connection to Byron, but Caroline was at the same time beginning to value the friendship rather than courtship of men such as the musician. It was the sense of direction guided by creative talent which appealed to her.

In April 1816 Lord Byron left his wife and baby daughter. He went abroad in a horrible cloud of evil innuendo, as it seemed forever. A brief verse of farewell – 'And if forever still forever fare thee well' – summed up the interlude, as it had turned out to be, in his life. It included a poignant allusion to the child Ada: 'wilt thou teach her to say "father", though his care she must forego'.

Glenarvon was published very shortly afterwards on 9 May 1816.[10]

The novel is set in Ireland, a country in which Caroline never saw Byron but which she visited at that crucial moment when her Anglo-Irish family dragged her away to their estates to make sure of ending the relationship. As we have seen, this was a period of great disturbance in Ireland; memories of the rebellion known as the Ninety-Eight, in which France had supported the Irish in their fight for independence, were still vivid. Lord Glenarvon himself is a rebel, and a rebel leader who addresses his fellow countrymen thus: '"Irishmen," said Glenarvon, throwing his dark mantle off, and standing amidst the grotesque and ferocious rabble, like some God from a higher world – "Irishmen, our country shall soon be free . . . the national Flag – the sacred green, shall fly over the ruins for ever . . .".'

His first appearance to Lady Calantha Delaval, however, shows him to be something much darker and stranger than that. Calantha hears the soft sounds of music and 'as if in a dream' follows the sound till she beholds a youth, leaning against a tree playing the lute. She gazes 'for one moment upon his countenance – she marked it. It was one of those faces which, having once beheld, we never afterwards forget. It seemed as if the soul of passion had been stamped and printed upon every feature. The eye beamed into life as it threw up its dark, ardent gaze, with a look nearly of inspiration, while the proud curl of the upper lip expressed haughtiness and bitter contempt; yet, even mixed with these fierce characteristic feelings, an air of melancholy and dejection shaded and softened every harsher expression.' Calantha felt the power, 'not then alone,' adds the author, 'but ever more'.

When she makes out the stranger's words, they are not exactly reassuring:

The mind has trac'd its own career,
Nor follow'd blind, where others trod
Nor, mov'd by love, or hope or fear
Ever bent to man or worshipp'd God

Gradually Glenarvon is established in the baleful Gothic tradition which includes not only the Wandering Jew, but the vampire who howls and barks 'whenever the moon shines bright'. And there are murders, mysteries, missing persons enough to satisfy the most lusty Gothic fancier. One might say that Caroline shows herself to be a nineteenth-century Agatha Christie as Glenarvon himself will turn out in the end to have another chilling identity, and a crucial missing person, assumed dead, will return.

There are in fact three heroines: Lady Calantha Delaval, Elinor St Clare and Alice MacAllain. Calantha herself is the daughter of the Duke of Altramonte, who has no son; thus his intended heir is his sister's son William Buchanan, and it is further planned in aristocratic fashion that Calantha shall marry her cousin. The potential match begins badly: Calantha much dislikes the 'cold, reserved' Buchanan. Even less to her taste is his mother, Lady Margaret. In spite of crafty smiles and highly polished manners, she is 'a dark intriguing spirit' (shades of Lady Melbourne). Then the plot twists as the Duchess of Altramonte gives birth to a son – thus excluding Buchanan from the inheritance. At which point Lady Margaret commissions one of her lovers, named Count Viviani, to arrange the murder of the baby . . . 'Mourn for the master's child is dead,' comes the terrible cry, and the Duchess his mother dies of grief.

Both Elinor St Clare, an Irish patriot, and the maiden Alice are involved with Glenarvon and die tragically in consequence. It is in Calantha that Caroline gives the most vivid self-portrait, although Elinor St Clare also has something of her fierce temperament. It is Elinor, placed in a convent where her aunt is Abbess after her betrayal, who cries 'Death to Glenarvon'. Calantha however shows remarkable self-knowledge. 'Thoughts, swift as lightning hurried upon her brain, projects seducing but visionary crowded upon her view: without a curb she followed the impulse of her feelings; and those feelings varied with every varying interest and impression: with disgust from the slavish followers of prejudice, she disdained the beaten track.' On the other hand Calantha is courageous: 'Your Calantha will never acknowledge a master [or] bow my unbroken spirit to that stern despot, whose only object is power and command,' she declares at one point.

Then there is the question of Calantha's marriage, her side of the story, as it were, being told to the Melbourne family, including that emotional remembrance of her wedding night: 'Calantha,' she writes, 'in manner, in appearance, in every feeling was but a child.' This innocent is duly married off to Lord Avondale and introduced to another world. Caroline Lamb manages to paint a vivid picture of a degenerate society – Whig Society – into which she is introduced, with Melbourne House as Monteith.

The main tragic drama is that of Glenarvon and Calantha. There are letters exchanged, some of which were based on Byron's original letters, adapted for the purpose by Caroline. One notable example is his letter of dismissal during his affair with Lady Oxford (in which she was invoked, but not named), including the deadly phrase: 'I love another.'[11] This was obviously a dangerous course for an author to pursue in the lifetime of the original letter-writer – and his supporters. At one point there is even a fake wedding ceremony under the light of the moon. None of this leads to anything but tragedy.

Unintentionally perhaps, Calantha's husband Lord Avondale emerges by the end as the hero of the story, or at any rate their married love endures. From the start Avondale, notwithstanding his lack of religious principle and his mocking sophistication – the qualities which corrupt his innocent wife – is an engaging figure, as though Caroline couldn't help flattering her husband William Lamb, despite intending to feature the devilish Byron-Glenarvon. The young Calantha is delighted with her marriage to him and adores their child. When she is contemplating running away to Glenarvon, she knows that Avondale's family will be more than happy. 'But there was one voice which still recalled her – it was her child's. "My boy will awake and find me gone – he shall never have to reproach his mother."' There were clearly echoes here of Caroline's own feelings about Byron – and Augustus.

Glenarvon himself meets a horrible fate, throwing himself off a ship and, despite rescue, sinking into death. As a lover and also as a patriot he has betrayed everyone and brought tragedy where he might have brought love. The patriotic betrayal is almost the worst: he actually goes to work for the British.

Glenarvon is thus a tale of love, certainly, but also essentially a story of betrayal, both political and romantic. It is an astonishing achievement for a first novel by a young woman well enough educated by the standards of her class but without the learning given to her male contemporaries at Harrow or Eton. The real force behind it was the active intelligence of Lady Caroline Lamb, restless with the limited opportunities offered by the life into which she had been born, ever seeking the satisfaction and comfort of creation.

Glenarvon was an immediate wild success. At this point Caroline felt she had had enough. She then wrote to Henry Colburn on the subject, adding: 'I . . . now wish to be done with the whole thing – it is useless to deny it – everyone knows who wrote the Book – make therefore what use you choose of it . . .'.[12]

But where the novel was concerned, Lady Caroline Lamb was not to be granted her wish: she would never be done with the whole thing. The publication of *Glenarvon*, from which there was no return, changed the life of its author forever. At least there was a new passion in her life – the passion for the writing, even if she had further embroiled herself in the old one.

CHAPTER NINE

================

Poor Calantha!

'Poor Calantha! What has she done? Observe that there are just now a great many people going about the world abusing her, and you should not give her up without being quite certain you have cause.'

Duke of Wellington to Mrs Arbuthnot,
20 July 1816

N O AUTHOR'S NAME was given for *Glenarvon*. In spite of – or because of – this it went rapidly through an enviable four editions. The first run of 1,500 copies sold out at once. It was symbolic of its success that the novelist Edward Bulwer-Lytton, a precocious reader in his early teens, noted in his own edition of the novel that when he read it at school, it left a deeper impression on him than any romance he remembered.[1] Caroline however did discover (or decide) that there were errors to be corrected between the first and second editions, as well as the argument about the songs and Isaac Nathan. An unpleasant allusion to Samuel Rogers was removed and references to Lady Holland as the Princess of Madagascar, about which Caroline had warned her lightly some time earlier, were toned down.

If the sales were tumultuous, the critical reaction was savage. Hobhouse, Byron's friend, summed it up when he referred to the 'little vicious author'. The distinguished Irish novelist Maria Edgeworth was a less prejudiced critic in theory, although even here we must bear in mind that Caroline had criticised her English-set novel *Patronage* to John Murray and claimed she had been unable to finish it because of its depiction of 'vulgar mediocre life'; at any rate Maria Edgeworth read two volumes before declaring: 'I cannot wade any further through blood and nonsense.' She also suspected another hand had written certain passages: Sydney Morgan, for example. Only the poetry was reckoned to be '*beautiful*' (her emphasis) with the inevitable comment: like Thomas Moore or Lord Byron. Basically, however, Maria Edgeworth thought *Glenarvon* 'too absurd' to do mischief.[2]

This was not the line taken by the Melbourne family. One of the side effects of the publication of *Glenarvon* was to enhance the determination of the Lambs to secure William's official Separation from Caroline. Various incidents during this period helped to make up a picture of lethal instability, easily manipulated in the agile fingers of Lady Melbourne and Emily.

There was, for example, the famous episode which Caroline called 'my *fracas* with the page' . . . not Caroline the page this time, but her own page, whom she called a little mischief, with a habit of throwing fireworks into the fire. Lord Melbourne scolded Caroline for this – and she scolded the boy. Until one day they were playing ball together and the boy threw a squib into the fire. Whereupon Caroline threw the ball at his head. Unfortunately it hit him on the temple and he bled. The page cried out: 'Oh, my lady, you have killed me!' In Caroline's own words, 'Out of my senses, I flew into the hall, and screamed: "Oh God, I have murdered the page!"'[3] The servants and people in the streets caught the sound, and news of the incident was soon spread about.

Ironically, the Lambs had other quarrels with their daughter-in-law for being too easy with her servants, too thoughtful about their comfort. In fact, 'no offers, no entreaties' could persuade the mischievous page himself to leave his mistress, despite her alleged 'barbarous' treatment of him.[4] In general she was a warm and thoughtful employer, as the page himself was aware – if sometimes too warm. After all, she had disagreed with William over an open carriage for a maid, considerate behaviour by later standards, but in the eyes of the Lambs confirming her as a tiresome daughter-in-law.

What did William himself think of the book? Caroline gave an agonising account of his reaction in a letter to Lord Granville, her mother's erstwhile lover, as she appealed for the support of the cousins with whom she had been brought up: 'I cannot bear not to see Harriet [Harryo] and Georgiana.' She told Granville: 'Wm Lamb heard of the novel the day it came out. I solemnly assure you upon my honour this passed between us. At first he was horrified: "Caroline, I have stood your friend till now – I even think you ill used; but if it is true this Novel is published – and as they say, against us all – I will never see you more." But then the critics and others wrote, happily for me, with such malignant violence that they over did it. He read what was termed a libel. He saw and feels, deeply feels, the unpleasant situation it is for him, but he loves me enough to stand firm as a rock, and to despise such as came forward to ruin one who had never hurt them.' She added what might have been her own proud motto: 'Recollect that when we fight for life and liberty we are not prudent.'⁵ William had put up with the defence of Lord Byron by his mother and sister for four years; but in the end, as ever, he was on Caroline's side.

This does not mean that William did more than tolerate what had happened; there is no certainty that he actually read the book: he may have listened to the hostile accounts of his mother and sister and instinctively ducked further confrontation with the notorious work. Later Caroline came to gloss over the scene in her account to her friend Lady Morgan: 'When the work was printed, I sent it to William Lamb. He was delighted with it; and we became united, just as the world thought we were parted for ever.'⁶

This optimistic view is contradicted by William himself writing to Lord Holland to apologise for not visiting him: it was 'the embarrassment' of 'the late events', which gave him 'great trouble and vexation, and produced an unwillingness to see anybody', particularly those who had been the object of an attack – he meant Lady Holland featured as the Princess of Madagascar. 'I did not write, because, what could I say? I could only exculpate myself from any previous knowledge, the effect of which must be to throw a heavier burden on the offending party' – meaning Caroline. As ever William showed himself the protector. His internal reflection was probably closer to what he told Queen Victoria many years later: 'No woman should touch pen and ink; they had too much passion and too little sense.' This was the pre-vailing view about female accomplishments: ladies should busy themselves graciously with sketches and Commonplace Books. The happy pencil which sketched was more suitable to their sex than the emotional pen which wrote. A recent study has in fact pointed out that Caroline was also an adept and inventive artist showing real talent.[7]

But as ever she refused to be confined and curtailed by the perceived limitations of her sex.

What was undoubtedly true about Caroline's happy statement to Lady Morgan is that William and Caroline remained appar-ently united in the wake of the publication of *Glenarvon*. The fact that the outraged world of High Society turned against her would if anything encourage William in that tender loyalty which was such an estimable part of his character. Sarah Lady Jersey, for example, saw to it that Lady Caroline Lamb was banned from Almack's, a mark of public disgrace which could not be missed. Lady Holland turned her back. There were individuals who were kind, such as Lady Salisbury, as Caroline noted, but in general she was in disgrace.

If one questions the basis of this disgrace, it clearly does not lie in the mere fact of writing a novel, 'my sole comfort' as Caroline called it. Women – ladies – wrote novels; this was Jane Austen's heyday, with *Pride and Prejudice* published in 1813 and *Emma* in 1815. It was the obvious connection with Lord Byron, calling attention to Caroline's famous romance, which outraged the grand Whig ladies, themselves involved in endless extramarital affairs, to say nothing of mothering children by their lovers. She refused to abide by the Whig code of maximum discretion – and maximum dissipation.

There was one, perhaps surprising supporter of *Glenarvon* who understood this very well: Annabella Lady Byron. It has been suggested by one authority that it may have been 'Caroline's grasp of Byron's character' which most impressed her about the novel, which she commended to others. Certainly Annabella was quick to point out the hypocrisy of the ladies who denounced it. 'Lady C. Lamb was at Anglesea House the other night and nobody spoke to her. I cannot help pitying her, for She must See around & *near* her so many whose Hypocrisy only has Secured them from Similar Scorn.'[8]

One person who in his own wry way did prove a support was Caroline's new admirer, the Duke of Wellington. In July, back in Paris, he wrote to his chief epistolary friend Mrs Harriet Arbuthnot: 'Poor Calantha!' as he persistently described her. 'What has she done? Observe that there are just now a great many people going about the world abusing her, and you should not give her up without being quite certain that you have cause.' And he continued to show an interest, grumbling in October: 'When you see Calantha tell her that I am very much offended with her for not having written to me once since my Departure from England!' Mrs Arbuthnot evidently carried out his instruction, for in November the Duke was able to tell her of Calantha's 'comical' letter to him: 'She says she is grown quite steady; but I suspect from the contents of the note that she boasts without cause; or at any rate the amendment is temporary.'[9]

Caroline Lamb duly sent *Glenarvon* to the Duke and he reported the gift to Harriet Arbuthnot: 'I have today received from her [Calantha] the third Edition of Glenarvon bound and ornamented with Black, that is in deep mourning, with an Inscription which I will shew you when we meet but all in Character.' The teasing hand-written dedication actually reads:

> 'From the Author
> Who is no more like Calantha
> than black Cap is'

The allusion 'black Cap' probably refers to Mrs Arbuthnot herself, famously upright and judgemental, hence the black cap of a judge; the nickname occurs once or twice in the Duke's correspondence.[10] The idea of Mrs Arbuthnot being the original of Calantha was obviously ludicrous.*

The Duke of Wellington maintained his friendship during the difficult times which, as he had predicted, now lay ahead for 'Calantha'. He saw her for example in November 1817 when he was briefly in London. The result was a scene which certainly did not detract from the picture the Melbournes were building up of her blatant 'madness', requiring some kind of restraining action – including separation from William.

'I saw Calantha the day when I was in London,' he related to Mrs Arbuthnot. 'Ridiculous scene when Lord Castlereagh is announced. Caroline was in a mighty taking, swore that she would lose her Reputation & wanted to conceal herself!' It ended with Castlereagh's brother Gerald Stewart escorting Lady Caroline to her carriage, while she scolded him for not retiring into another room, so that she could stay a little longer with the Duke. Nevertheless, whatever Caroline Lamb's eccentricities, the Duke maintained his friendship with 'Calantha'.[11]

Then there was the key figure in it all: Lord Byron himself. Byron's marriage was in ruins: the Deed of Separation was signed on 21 April 1816. Of 'the rumours of which I was Subject' surrounding the end of his marriage, Byron would observe two years later with his usual morbid wit: 'If *they were true*, I was unfit for England, if *false*, England is unfit for me.'[12] At all events he left England in April, shortly before the publication of *Glenarvon*.

On his European travels, he could not however leave behind the torrential gossip which the allegedly anonymous novel provoked. It was Madame de Staël in her salon on the shores of Lake

---

* The volumes are still to be seen in the Duke of Wellington's library at Stratfield Saye stamped with 'W' beneath the ducal coronet; there is a blot on the 't' of 'Author' and the word 'Calantha' veers downward, being too long to fit the page.

Geneva at the Château de Coppet who asked him the question to which everyone wanted to know the answer: was he the original of Lord Glenarvon? Lord Byron's answer was diplomatic: it was possible, but he had never posed for the portrait. Madame de Staël proceeded to lend him her copy. At which point Byron came up with a terse but expressive comment: 'I read "Glenarvon", too, by Caro Lamb. *God damn!*'

This after all was the kind of episode from which Byron was always going to emerge the cool winner: as when Caroline left the words 'Remember me' on his desk followed by his lethal poetic rejoinder. In a subsequent comment to his friend Thomas Moore on the subject of *Glenarvon*, he elaborated: 'It seems to me, that if the authoress had written the *truth*, and nothing but the truth – the whole truth – the romance would not only have been more *romantic*, but more entertaining. As for the likeness, the picture can't be good – I did not sit long enough.'[13]

Byron's friends left behind in England, such as Hobhouse, now took up the cudgels on his behalf. Hobhouse noted in his diary on 9 May: 'Glenarvon – the hero – is a monster & meant for B . . . I called on the bitch & was asked whether any harm had been done by the book . . . she also showed me half bawdy pictures of hers of B.' Wrangling ensued in which Hobhouse's threats of publication of Caroline's letters to Byron, sent via Lady Melbourne, were met by formidable counter-threats by Caroline: 'let him but publish the tenthpart of a single line in any letter I ever wrote to him . . . and if I die for it I vow to God I will on the instant publish not only all his, but the whole exact journal I have kept of my acquaintance with him, and his conduct during the last four years'.[14] Caroline had of course already used Byron's terrible letter of dismissal – 'I love another' – in the text of *Glenarvon.**

---

* The original sent by Byron is printed in his *Letters & Journals*, although the text only exists in *Glenarvon*; the editor gives as his reason for its inclusion that 'Byron did not question its authenticity when he read the book; he must have recognised the substance of what he had written'.[15]

Her real feelings about her work and Byron were summed up when Caroline told Hobhouse, in response to his accusations that she was ruining Byron: the novel might be 'stupid', might be 'unseemly' for her to write, but was 'assuredly anything but malevolent'.[16] This was true. Caroline Lamb wanted to attest to the passion she had once felt – and Byron had felt too. As a writer, this was her chosen mode of expression. But she was looking for the world to accept her testimony; she was not looking for revenge.

Byron himself was far away from these particular wranglings. In any case in Italy, on his way to Greece, he had become involved with Teresa Guiccoli, a relationship which has been described as 'the Last Attachment'. A period in Venice followed. Yet Caroline was not forgotten. Images of her did not entirely fade from his life, as she who could not bear to be ignored would probably have been happy to know, despite their equivocal nature; it might have provided comfort for the attacks of Hobhouse and Lady Melbourne.

When he first got to know Teresa Guiccoli Byron described her to Douglas Kinnaird as 'a sort of Italian Caroline Lamb, except she is much prettier, and not so savage. But she has the same red-hot head – the same noble dis*dain* [sic] of public opinion.' He also made the comparison to his half-sister Augusta: 'the Guiccoli was romantic . . . in short she was a kind of Caroline Lamb – but very pretty and gentle'. This did not stop him lending Teresa his own copy of *Glenarvon* and then going on to complain that 'your little head is heated now by that damned novel', a reaction that was presumably expected and led him on to fulminate about the author 'in every country and at all times my evil Genius'.[17]

Later, when things were not so good between Byron and Teresa Guiccoli, as his planned departure to Greece did not include her, he once again made the comparison to Douglas Kinnaird as he moaned: if Teresa made a scene, 'we shall have another romance – and a tale of ill usage and abandonment – and Lady Caroling [sic] and Lady Byroning – and Glenarvoning . . . there never was a man who gave up so much for women – and all I have gained by it – has been the character of treating them badly'.[18]

*

There were two stresses in the life of Caroline Lamb at this time – additional to the furore caused by her novel, and the ambitions of William's family to get rid of her. The first was her own troubled health. Caroline appeared to have a fluttering heart which by the autumn made the doctor very uneasy. She told her mother-in-law how she had been given a 'huge blister which gave me great pain bigger than this paper over the whole side & today he thinks of bleeding me'.*[19] Meantime the heart 'fluttering and beating' affected her so much that she felt like someone with asthma. She added, significantly: 'I do not find Laudanum or Ether or Valerian of the least use.'[20] As has been seen, such drugs as laudanum were regularly prescribed at this period and taken by varied users who would not be regarded as addicts. But for the future it was notable that laudanum was becoming a regular part of Caroline's distressed life.

The second stress was provided by the continuing problem of her son, who celebrated his ninth birthday in August 1816. Shortly afterwards Caroline wrote in despair to Lady Melbourne: 'You will not wonder . . . that I should feel almost heart broken about Augustus I really am so dispirited I scarce know what to do he has 4 attacks today 2 very very severe ones.' The doctor was going to give him a 'cleaning dose'. Then Caroline proposed to take him to Brighton; 'if William can spare me I shall go too'.[21] All sorts of treatments were tried to prevent or alleviate his fits: for a while 'blistering' in his case seemed to work.

The following year, a step was taken towards his education which would seem to indicate progress was possible – at least mental progress. A certain Dr Robert Lee was engaged in November 1817 and proceeded to teach him, for five years, not only reading and writing but also Greek and Latin. The fact that Dr Lee went on to become Regius Professor at Glasgow University demonstrates that Augustus was considered capable

---

* Blistering was a medical treatment which involved placing hot plasters on to the skin to raise blisters, which were then drained.

of learning, despite his physical weaknesses, the combination of size, ungainliness and rumbustious behaviour: he saw 'rolling the maids about' as a form of jolly joke.[22] All this would lead to Emily Lamb in future years making the unfortunate comparison to Mary Shelley's monster in *Frankenstein*, having just seen the monster enacted on stage: 'the huge creature without sense put us all in mind of Augustus'.[23]

But Caroline loved 'her boy'. And although William, whether by design or the different pattern of a man's life, saw much less of him, there is no reason to suppose that he supported those who wished to confine Augustus to some institution (of which plenty existed).

Compared to these real torments, the efforts of the Lamb family to limit the damage, as they saw it, by a legal Separation seems to have caused Caroline much less agitation. As time passed, it is clear that she felt a kind of confidence in her husband which gave her courage, even when Society in general regarded her with distaste and the Melbournes in particular made humiliating efforts to secure her at Brocket Hall under the care of two strong female nurses.

One short scene in the summer of 1816 symbolised the impenetrable union of William and Caroline. Legal papers of Separation had been prepared. William gave in to his mother's determination and weakly agreed. Lady Melbourne went down to Brocket to supervise the final process. On arrival she found her son and his wife at breakfast.[24]

'William, some more muffin?' she heard Caroline say in that unmistakeable Cavendish drawl learnt in childhood. The couple were the picture of happiness. There was to be no Separation.

In December 1816 Harryo related with a mixture of indignation and admiration to her brother Hart how she had gone with Granville to Melbourne House to call upon her. 'Following the page through the dark and winding passages to the William Lambs' "upper apartments" I was received with rapturous embraces, and tremendous spirits. I expected she would have put on an appearance of something, but to do her justice she only displayed a total want of shame and consummate impudence, which, whatever they may be in themselves, are at least better or less disgusting than pretending or acting a more interesting part.'

Harryo was then dragged to the unresisting William and dismissed. 'I looked as I felt stupefied. And this is the guilty, broken-hearted Calantha who could only expiate her crimes with death.'[25]

It remained to be seen whether there was another possible existence for this real-life Calantha or whether the continued memories of the real-life Glenarvon would ultimately destroy it. It was clear that the noble Lord Avondale figure of William Lamb was not going to effect the destruction.

PART FOUR

THE WISH TO LIVE

'Now nothing vexes me – for I value nothing. I am concerned about nothing for I possess nothing . . . for what I did wrong I have long since repented . . . I wish to live for I am truly happy.'

An old lady on the Brocket estate in praise of age,
quoted by Caroline Lamb, 1817

CHAPTER TEN

Come to Brocket Hall

'Adieu, whenever it pleases you come and see me at Brocket Hall. If you have a moment to spare . . .'

Lady Caroline Lamb to Ugo Foscolo, 1817

COMPARED TO THE sophisticated rigours of Melbourne House in Whitehall, under the eyes of Caroline Lamb's mother-in-law, Brocket Hall in Hertfordshire offered simpler, pastoral pleasures. 'Poor Calantha' was shunned in London but at Brocket she could perhaps lead another kind of calmer life.

Here at Brocket could take place the treatment of Augustus, even the remaining intimacies of the Lambs' marriage, in comparative obscurity. Caroline could enjoy riding wildly round the park to soothe her mercurial spirit: as has been stressed, she rode astride, scorning the contemporary lady's position of side-saddle. Her tender inclination towards caring for other people – the other side of her character which contrasted with her notorious exhibitionism – could find fulfilment in village life and the other pursuits of landlords with their tenantry.

One feature of the Lambs' life there was the series of children or young people who were, in a manner of speaking, adopted by Caroline. There were no further children of the marriage. The most likely explanation lies in the fact Caroline's earlier experiences with childbearing left her physically unable to conceive; there is no reason to suppose that all sexual relations with her husband ceased. Although the second-hand testimony of the courtesan Harriette Wilson in her scurrilous *Memoirs*, via a former maid of Caroline Lamb, must be treated with caution, she does tell a plausible story of Caroline pestering her husband: 'I must and will come into your bed. I am your lawful wife. Why am I to sleep alone?' It is easy to imagine a scene like this happening. On the other hand, the maid's tittle-tattle about Lady Caroline and Augustus's resident carer, Dr Lee, a story of her stocking left in his bed, is implausible. It was however easy and enjoyable for servants living close to their mistress to invent stories and still more enjoyable for Harriette Wilson, who had nothing to lose, to repeat them.[1]

In an age before effective contraception, it is also notable that Caroline, unlike her mother, aunt and mother-in-law, never produced a child allegedly fathered by a lover. It has therefore been plausibly suggested that this void, coupled with the continuing sad state of Augustus, left both William and Caroline in need of satisfying their parental instincts.[2]

There were the pages, always Caroline's special care, given her early self-identification with the role. Of course the introduction of young people into her household was not an untroubled pursuit: especially as at one point Caroline took to picking them up casually on the shore of the lake. She explained herself thus: her behaviour was the result of 'an idle whim of mine more for educating a boy and having something to do than any other motive'. The girls were easier to absorb into the household; over the years numbers of them came and went, most prominently one named Susan Churchill, the illegitimate daughter of the young, unmarried Harriet Spencer, a relation of Caroline on her mother's side. Lady Bessborough gave Susan a home. It was not absolutely clear who her father was, except that he was a member of the Churchill family headed by the Duke of Marlborough.[3]

When Lady Bessborough died, Caroline applied herself to the needs of little Susan, who was three, with enthusiasm, and as a result gave her what has been described as 'the happy gift of a secure early childhood'.[4] In bringing Susan up, Caroline was in a sense continuing the tradition of her female relations in their tangled history of 'fatherless' children and adopting families. Susan easily found her place in the Brocket establishment, with its dogs, its horses, its friendly maids and its chef, oddly named Napoleon, listed in the accounts as Mr Napoleon of Paris. For company there were plenty of children under Caroline's benevolent patronage, including the children of doctors brought in to tend to Augustus. And there was Augustus himself, who, despite being eleven years old, always seemed like a toddler.

It was helpful that Brocket Hall was (and remains) set in a peculiarly attractive position, aloft on a little hill above a lake set in a roaming green and leafy park. Unlike Melbourne Hall in Derbyshire, the house was not too far from London itself for casual visiting: a mere twenty-five miles whereas Melbourne Park in contrast was 120 miles away. There were neighbours, such as the Marquess of Salisbury and his wife, at Hatfield House. Caroline also began to develop the agreeable habit of asking friends to stay: not any old friends, and not Lord Byron (far away if not forgotten in Italy), but intelligent people who for one reason or other attracted her interest.

Of course, even life at Brocket was not the total Paradise which Caroline sought. Emily, her sister-in-law, now married to Earl Cowper, took malicious pleasure in reporting the total failure of one planned-to-be-lavish dinner party where no genuine guests turned up, and the company was restricted to children including Augustus and Dr Lee and 'four strangers'.* 'The whole House was lighted up, there were several supper tables, a band of twenty-four musicians . . . The expense of these failures is as great as if she had succeeded,' pointed out Emily. 'In a concern of this sort she doesn't mind what she

---

* The humiliation endured by the hosts of such parties has sometimes provided the plot for novelists including Evelyn Waugh in his short story 'Bella Fleace Gave a Party' (1934). Here the solution is found after Bella Fleace's death – in the shape of a wadge of undelivered invitations. The problem with Caroline Lamb's party was the hostess, not the invitations.

throws away – but means to make up for it the next week by the most miserable stinginess.' Emily added: 'There never was such a woman!'[5]

As for the husband of this woman, William Lamb was returned to Parliament after a gap of four years. Now he was the MP for Peterborough in Cambridgeshire. In 1814 he had declared absence from Westminster to be 'utter extinction and annihilation'. Nevertheless, William was not prepared for that docile agreement with his Whig relations which would guarantee advancement. He had added stubbornly that, much as he wished for a seat in the Commons, 'I could not accept any but a perfectly Independent one,' and could not bind himself to follow any political party or leader currently in either House of Parliament.[6] This attitude – strangely lofty as it might seem, in a young man of political ambitions – coupled with his notorious wife, meant that his mother and sister Emily Cowper muttered angrily at his lack of advancement and inevitably focused on the notorious wife as the prime obstacle. A legal Separation remained their joint aim.

That was certainly not the aim of Lady Caroline Lamb. Quite worldly enough to appreciate the disaster she had made of her public life, she was also quite romantic enough to wish to live on in the style to which she had become accustomed, as the object of love of William Lamb. She was distressed when she had to spend their twelfth wedding anniversary on 3 June 1817 alone. There remained Whig Society. She might be shunned in London, but she did not shun London. In the ideal life she planned for herself in her reflective moments there might be some combination of city and country, in both of which she would achieve some kind of happiness.

Caroline's Parisian admirer Michael Bruce was back in London, following that period in prison as a punishment for his escapade freeing Napoleon's supporter Lavalette. To him she confided what she considered her new state of mind. One letter she quoted to him with admiration concerned an eighty-year-old woman living on the Brocket estate who had told her that the last thirty years were the happiest of her life: 'for now nothing vexes me – for

I value nothing. I am concerned about nothing for I possess nothing . . . for what I did wrong I have long since repented . . . I wish to live for I am truly happy . . .'. And so on. The implication was that in her early thirties Caroline Lamb was reaching or had reached that happy philosophic state. Although the end of the letter would not have helped to convince Bruce.

Caroline reverted to the subject of Byron: 'God grant him His blessing and forgiveness – I cannot mine no not even in Death.' Her continuing bitterness seeped away at the end of the letter: 'do tell me why you say he is ill – after all I trust in God he is not ill'.[7]

One of Caroline's more satisfactory new friends was Ugo Foscolo, an Italian writer of distinction: he was thirty-nine in 1817. If Caroline unconsciously looked for some connection to the lost Byron in her friends, with Foscolo it was intellectual rather than physical. A contemporary described him as 'small, wiry and highly animated, with a sensuous mouth and a hot temper'.[8] A portrait by François-Xavier Fabre, a few years before he came to England, shows a handsome, wiry man, but with the sensuous mouth well in evidence.

Foscolo's father was an impoverished Italian nobleman and his mother Greek, part of his childhood being spent in Venice, from where he went to the University of Padua. As a young man he supported Napoleon in the creation of a free Venetian republic, writing a poem *To Bonaparte the liberator* in 1797. He volunteered for the French army and was made prisoner, all the time writing. In 1807 appeared his great poem *Dei Sepolcri*, in which the mighty dead of the past were summoned from their tombs to fight for their country. Plays as well as poetry followed, while Foscolo progressed from Milan until the arrival of the Austrians caused him to move on, finally reaching England at the end of 1816.

Immediately Foscolo became a star in literary London, writing for the *Edinburgh Review* and the *Quarterly Review*, while Lord Holland gave him his approval in double-edged terms: 'His learning and vivacity are wonderful, and he seems to have great elevation of mind, and to be totally exempt from affectation, tho' perhaps not equally so from enthusiasm, violence and resentment.'[9] Only Foscolo's finances were disastrous, leading to a spell in a debtor's prison on the one hand, and on the other a rather more respectable post teaching Italian at a Quaker School. When it came to women Foscolo might not have looked like Byron; but he had no trouble attracting them, especially older women, and for many years was the lover of Countess Antonietta Fagnani Arese, sometimes compared to the English courtesan Harriette Wilson.

But a lover was not what Caroline Lamb sought at the present time; she was reaching out to the kind of literary life (with herself included as a writer) where men such as Foscolo provided interesting company. It was the same instinct which had led her to enjoy her contacts with the composer Isaac Nathan from the start. There was furthermore a certain glamour about Foscolo, based on his foreign background and its connections to Byron, which she liked. (Foscolo in his turn was attracted, like other men in the future, to the idea of the woman who had been the famous Byron's mistress.) If she wanted emotional torments, there was the continuing consequences of 'that moment' in the shape of arguments with Byron's friends and publisher about correspondence between the pair.

As it was she happily pursued Foscolo, calling herself 'Votre Agneau', sending him her drawings and inviting him on visits, beginning with Melbourne House. He read to her from his translation of *The Iliad*. Later she visited him at his Regent's Park residence, Digamma Cottage, having searched for it with difficulty, despite William being in attendance. And Foscolo gave her brisk literary advice which the admirers of Lady Caroline Lamb would feel was inappropriate, while her detractors would consider essential: 'write a book which will offend nobody – women cannot afford to shock'.[10]

One pleading letter in November 1817 makes their relationship clear: Foscolo might not think the drawings good enough for him, but she hoped he would visit her anyway – 'and that is what I should like. I am sure, however, that walking will not be good for you, allow my carriage, that has nothing to do, to convey you here. I am going to the theatre this evening, would you like to come or would you rather take tea tomorrow? I am alone and I should so enjoy listening to Homer . . .'.[11]

Another letter tries to smooth over a tiff at a party when Foscolo appears to have left her side, with the invitation: 'whenever it pleases you come and see me at Brocket Hall'. And a significant note was struck to make it clear this was not a love letter: 'William admires you and if I am worth nothing, he is worth a great deal.' An invitation to take refuge in a place of his own in their neighbourhood followed: 'There is a small place near us at Brocket on a height near no water not expensive very pretty and comfortable very convenient if you would like to have it.' The letter ended on the usual imploring: 'I am at home all day, my carriage has nothing to do, if you would like to come here this evening, we shall be delighted but I will not permit you to walk home.'[12]

Meanwhile Caroline's friendship with Isaac Nathan continued and undoubtedly brought her great pleasure. Caroline and William became godparents to his daughter Louisa Caroline Nathan. And Isaac Nathan would give testimony later to Caroline's disinterested benevolence. One example occurred when she asked Nathan to help her over a concert 'for the benefit of a lady in distressed circumstances'. When Nathan proposed 'the powerful aid of Miss Love's rich voice', Caroline exclaimed: 'Oh! Do ask her to come – will my writing to her assist you?' And immediately sat herself down to do so. Nathan, expecting a letter, found himself with a picture of a kneeling Cupid with the caption: 'Love implores Love to come.'[13]

There were other literary friendships – or attempts at contacts, such as a letter Caroline wrote to Thomas Malthus over his book *An Essay on the Principle of Population*. Amelia Opie, the novelist, was invited to Brocket. There were of course what might be termed Byronic outbursts (although Byron himself would have called them Carolinish). How could there not? The most flamboyant occurred appropriately enough when the first two Cantos of Byron's great poem *Don Juan* were published by John Murray in 1819.[14] Byron dedicated the Cantos to 'Ianthe', in other words Charlotte Harley, the little daughter of his mistress Lady Oxford. Based on a Spanish character of legend, *Don Juan* was that delightful literary apparition, an immediate shocking success. The boy Juan is first introduced as: 'A little curly-headed, good-for-nothing', before his education elicits some enjoyably louche verses:

> His classic studies made a little puzzle,
> Because of filthy loves of gods and goddesses
> Who in the earlier ages raised a bustle,
> But never put on pantaloons or bodices . . .

Then Don Juan begins his love life early with a precocious affair with a married woman, until discovery leads to his expulsion to Cadiz. Shipwrecked on the way, he makes a landfall on one of the Cyclades islands, where two women, Haidée and her maid Zoe, nurture him; Haidée and Don Juan then fall in love, with dire consequences. Haidée's father enslaves the young Don Juan and sends him to Constantinople (part of the Ottoman Empire).

Throughout the poem, love is the subject of dark reflection, as in Canto II:

> Oh Love! Thou art the very god of evil,
> For, after all, we cannot call thee devil.

Don Juan certainly veers between being master and slave of love: sometimes he hates 'inconstancy' and at other times he succumbs to temptation:

> I saw the prettiest creature, fresh from Milan,
> Which gave me some sensations like a villain.

Despite – or because of – its success, the critical reception of the first two Cantos showed in some cases a ferocity of the type that the author himself was well capable of expressing. Byron was particularly angered by *Blackwood's Edinburgh Magazine*'s verdict of 'this filthy impious poem', since it was published by John

Murray himself. The author fared no better: he was described as 'an unrepenting, unsoftened, smiling, sarcastic, joyous sinner'. Byron protested to Murray: 'Your Blackwood accuses me of treating women harshly – it may be so – but I have been their martyr – My whole life has been sacrificed *to* them & *by* them.'[15]

It was never likely that such a sensational event as the publication of such a poem by Lord Byron would be ignored by Caroline Lamb, even the new Caroline bent on enjoying the charms of age, as outlined by the old lady on the Brocket estate. Her first response indicated the direction she felt her new life as a writer should take. Shortly after the publication of Cantos I and II of *Don Juan*, Lady Caroline Lamb came up with *A New Canto*.[16] This was published anonymously.*

The author has a merry time mixing references to the poem itself with satirical allusions to the poet. It begins,

> I'm sick of fame – I'm gorged with it – so full
> I almost could regret the happier hour
> When northern oracles proclaimed me dull,
> Grieving my Lord should so mistake his power –

Then there is a swipe at the magazine which had attacked *Don Juan*:

> Vile cheats! He knew not, impudent reviewer,
> Clear spring of Helicon from the common sewer.

The poem moves to Doomsday and has a splendid time with the demolition of St Paul's, starting with the Ball on the roof holding the Cross, which comes

> . . . tumbling with a lively crash
> And splits the pavement up, and shakes the shops,
> Teeth chatter, china dances, spreads the flash

---

* It is now accepted as her work: the editors of *The Works of Lady Caroline Lamb* offer persuasive evidence for Caroline as author.[17]

. . . the Bank of England stops;
Loyal and radical, discreet and rash,
Each on his knees in tribulation flops;
The Regent raves (Moore chuckling at his pain)
And sends about for ministers in vain.

The English countryside does not escape: the Peak of Derbyshire (an allusion to Hart's beloved Chatsworth) 'goes to and
fro', while back in London the Monument to the Great Fire of
London 'like drunken sot . . . is reeling'. The destruction passes
on to Europe, with a swipe at Paris, 'an odious place too, in
these modern times,/Small incomes, runaways and swindlers
eager', before becoming thick with allusions to *Don Juan* and
Byron himself: for example his predilection for Napoleon, who
never flinched at 'massacre or murder', is mocked. Finally the
spirit of Byron exclaims with an honesty he did not achieve at
the start:

Mad world! For fame we rant, call names and fight –
I scorn it heartily, yet love to dazzle it.

Whatever pleasure Caroline derived from writing her little
satire, she found occasion for another type of pleasure in 1820,
the year following publication of *Don Juan*. This was the pleasure of a public demonstration.

The death of Lady Melbourne in April 1818 had removed one
obstacle to an easy London life. In later years, Elizabeth Melbourne's rheumatism became an agonising condition, for which
she took refuge in the fashionable remedy of laudanum laced
with opium; the doses grew ever larger under the care of the
Prince Regent's physician Dr Richard Warren. Her sufferings
increased, and so did the doses. On 13 March she told her son
Fred Lamb that if she could write 'a word that I was released
from the pain I should be very happy'.[18]
Finally, on 6 April 1818, at the age of sixty-six, Lady Melbourne was released: she died at Melbourne House, and was

interred at Hatfield where her lost grandchildren, William and Caroline's babies, lay. Only the ghost of the vigilante mother-in-law on the ground floor would now keep watch on Caroline Lamb's comings and goings to the apartments above.

At this point Emily Cowper decided to get Caroline readmitted to Almack's, her expulsion having been a public token of her disgrace. As she told her brother Fred, sounding the usual note of scorn when writing about her sister-in-law (whom she called Calantha as in 'that infernal book'): 'She has been quieter lately, as her only object is to push herself on in this world, which is, I assure you, very uphill work, tho' William gives her all the help he can, and now, as he *will* stick to her, I think it better to give her any lift I can – for her disgrace only falls more or less on him.'[19]

Almack's had been wittily described by Horace Walpole as 'The Ladies' Club of both Sexes'.[20] The fact that Almack's was the only club in England which admitted women, and where women – women of the highest rank – exercised the controlling will over membership emphasised the female misogyny which was so often directed towards Caroline. As the Duke of Devonshire had said so long ago, men liked Lady Caroline better than women. Emily Cowper now enabled her sister-in-law to attend once more their celebrated parties in a ballroom capable of holding over 1,500 people. Among these parties were masquerades.

It was that sharp observer Harriette Wilson who noted in her *Memoirs* that 'she loved a masquerade because a female could never enjoy the same liberty anywhere else'.[21] Caroline promptly took advantage of her restored status by appearing at a masquerade at the club dressed up as Don Juan, attended by Devils, played by pages, with extra recruits from the Drury Lane Theatre to whom she appealed with this winning letter: 'I must have a Devil – could you come with me as such. I want a very dear Devil not in bad taste.' In the opinion of the *Morning Chronicle*, Caroline did not succeed in fulfilling this want: according to its report, repeated drilling by 'the Don' (i.e. Caroline) in private did not prevent the young Devils being 'determined to carry the whole crowd off to Tartarus by a *coup de main*'.[22]

The event was reported by John Murray to Byron himself, at this point in Ravenna and already heavily involved with that Caroline Lamb-lookalike Teresa Guiccoli. Byron's response came in the shape of a snarl: 'What you say of Lady Caroline Lamb's Juan at the Masquerade don't surprise me – I only wonder that She went so far as "the *Theatre*" for "*the Devils*" having them so much more natural at home – or if they were busy – she might have borrowed the bitch her Mother's – Lady Bessborough to wit – The hack whore of the last century.'[23]

Despite the slur implied by Byron's insults from afar, Caroline Lamb had been allowed to electioneer for George Lamb when he stood for Parliament in the spring of 1819. There was a Byronic twist here too. George Lamb, her brother-in-law and husband of the other Caroline (born St Jules), was standing at a by-election for the Westminster seat. His opponent – standing as a Radical as opposed to George Lamb's Whig – was John Cam Hobhouse, Byron's friend since Cambridge and frequent fellow traveller: ten years earlier he had accompanied him to Greece, among other countries, and written notes to Canto IV of *Childe Harold*. Caroline's celebrated aunt, Georgiana Duchess of Devonshire, had earlier shown herself to be a star at electioneering. But in any case this was the kind of occasion for which Caroline was by temperament ideally suited. It enabled her to display two things: first of all her deep, continuing loyalty to her husband, and secondly – herself.

So Caroline flung herself into the fray. As Georgiana had done, she exchanged kisses for votes; she showed her common touch by making her way into taverns and enjoying a drink – alcohol was something that was becoming increasingly important in her life. Caroline also employed her ready pen to solicit support. The philosopher William Godwin was among those she approached: 'Lady Caroline Lamb presents her compliments to Mr. Godwin, and fears his politics will incline him to refuse a request of his interest for Mr. George Lamb. She hopes, however, it will not offend if she solicits it.' To which Godwin gratifyingly replied: 'You have mistaken me. Mr. G. Lamb has my sincere good wishes. My creed is a short one. I am in principle a Republican but in practice a Whig.'[24] Their correspondence led in fact to an important friendship, as will be seen – and of course subsequent offers of hospitality at Brocket: 'Your room shall always be ready.'

The Westminster constituency at this point has been described as 'dominated by middle-class voters',[25] predominantly shop-keepers, tailors and the like. Opponents of the Whigs readily besmirched the character of Lady Caroline Lamb at this point; yet those same qualities of outgoing gaiety and high spirits which she undoubtedly possessed, for all her tribulations, meant that voters were amused and presumably in certain cases swayed. She herself protested against these tactics of denigration in a letter to Hobhouse. While aware that 'songs and squibs' were fair on each side, she asked him how he would have felt 'if any of our people were to vilify your Mother, your sisters . . . or any of the friends interested for you – every one has some vulnerable point, no human being in person and Character is wholly free from either ridicule or imputation . . .'.[26]

At all events George Lamb defeated Hobhouse. As a result, William's younger brother sat for the constituency for a year, until Hobhouse defeated him in March 1820 at the General Election caused by the death of George III. On this occasion, Lady Caroline was not permitted by the family to repeat her electioneering act. George Lamb, who had a separate career as a writer, returned to Parliament later as Member for Dungarvan until his death.

The original defeat of Hobhouse found Byron hissing from afar at the part played by Lady Caroline Lamb in terms which did him little credit. Although if Caroline was informed of Byron's rage, she could hardly have claimed that it was unjust. Hobhouse's connection to Byron surely played some part in her enthusiasm for George Lamb's success. Byron began by sympathising with Hobhouse – 'I had much at Heart in your gaining the Election' – before denouncing Caroline and explicitly outlining how he could have suppressed her. 'If I had guessed at your *opponent* . . . I would have f----d [*sic*] Caroline Lamb out of her "two hundred" votes although at the expense of a testicle – I

think I could have neutralized her zeal with a little management.'
Byron then proceeded to a tirade against the whole Lamb family
in equally gross terms: 'alas! who could have thought of that
whole Cuckoldy family's *standing* for *member* – I suppose it is
the first time George Lamb ever *stood* for anything . . .'.[27]

Byron's outraged loquacity from afar did little to damage Lady
Caroline Lamb. It was events closer to home which threatened.
On 11 November 1821, just before Caroline Lamb's thirty-sixth
birthday, she lost the family member who had meant most to her
in all her early life: her mother.

Caroline's brother Willy Ponsonby, for one, dreaded the effect
the news would have on his sister. In truth Harriet's health had
never been particularly good: there had been an early stroke in
1791 and other ailments; but her strong character had sustained
her for many years, until she died finally at the age of sixty. She
was in fact in Italy, having gone abroad in a party which included
an ailing grandchild. Unfortunately, little Henry Ponsonby, son
of Willy, died despite the care given him, including that of the
Empress Marie Louise's own doctor.[28] It was to Granville, her
ex-lover, that Harriet wrote of the tragedy of watching the 'beautiful boy, knowing that he cannot recover . . . his eyes brightly
fixed and beautiful, then fading away to the damp paleness of
death'. The Bessborough party proceeded on its journey but Harriet herself became seriously ill, increased by the sheer exhaustion
of day-and-night care for her grandson. Further felled by an agonising stomach condition, Harriet Bessborough died very shortly
after arrival in Florence.

No one could pretend that a woman who had contributed
twice to the celebrated – or notorious – 'Children of the Mist'
was a good wife. But Harriet Bessborough had been a good
mother, and extremely supportive of her tempestuous daughter
in her difficulties. On her deathbed one of her last thoughts had
been for Caroline, whom she described as 'the joy and torment
of my life', and she told Willy to give his sister the pink diamond
ring which had belonged to Caroline's beloved grandmother
Lady Spencer. She also sent a positive message about Augustus:
there was a certain doctor who had had fits up to the age of

fourteen or fifteen, and none after that, and was leading a normal intelligent life.

It was particularly tragic for Caroline Lamb that she could not even attend her mother's second funeral, which was held at Derby Cathedral, following a ceremony in Italy. This was to precede interment in the Cavendish vault, beside Harriet's sister Georgiana. Caroline got as far as Derby the night before, where she stayed with members of her family. During the night however she became agitated, as Hart recorded, and by morning she was so ill that she gave up being present. When she decided she wanted to visit the vault later in the day, Hart ordered the vault to be closed in order to prevent her. Ever protective, he feared for the effect it would have upon the vulnerable Caroline.

The fact was that Caroline's own health was declining, but for different reasons. This did not mean however that she had reached the last chapter of this life: whenever possible, in the words of the old lady at Brocket, she was determined to enjoy being alive. In spite of tragedy, in spite of illness, in spite of her notorious nervous temperament, there still might be books to write and new relationships to form so that the words 'Come to Brocket Hall' might still have meaning.

CHAPTER ELEVEN

Wreck of a Little Boat

'I am like the wreck of a little boat, for I never come up to the sublime and beautiful – merely a little gay merry boat, which perhaps stranded itself at Vauxhall or London Bridge – or wounded without killing itself as a butterfly does in a tallow candle.'

Lady Caroline Lamb to William Godwin

A YOUNG ADMIRER now entered the Brocket life of Lady Caroline Lamb. He would begin his suit with an ardent tribute.

Born in May 1803, Edward Bulwer was seventeen years younger than Caroline; he was the son of General Earle Bulwer and the heiress to Richard Warburton Lytton; his family lived in the neighbourhood at Knebworth in Hertfordshire; later he would attend Cambridge University (also not too far from Brocket). A precocious writer who had poems published at the age of fifteen, he would one day be celebrated as Lord Lytton, the author of many hugely popular novels such as *The Last Days of Pompeii* and author of the quotation with which Caroline Lamb would entirely have agreed: 'the Pen is mightier than the Sword'.

The idea of the famous Lady Caroline Lamb, the lover of Lord Byron, the author of *Glenarvon*, fascinated him, especially when he heard of her chivalrous behaviour towards the victim of an accident. Bulwer was impressed – and enchanted. It was indeed ironic that the rumours, myths and truth of the Byronic romance which smeared the reputation of Caroline Lamb in the world also provoked enormous, one might say competitive interest among other men.

Bulwer wrote her a poem dedicated to: 'Lady Caroline L. Who at the Sutton Hoo Races set a glorious example of her feeling & humanity when a poor Man being much hurt she had him conveyed to her own carriage and interested herself most charitably in his recovery.' The poem then proceeded to address Caroline as

> Daughter of Feeling, Queen of Love!
> Tis to thee these lines are due
> Beauteous as the Cyprian Dove
> Hast thou then her nature too . . .

It ended:

> My Guardian Angel hovering near
> Soar'd upwards with that deed of thine
> And as he dropp'd th' applauding Tear
> Wrote down the name of Caroline[1]

Bulwer's poem was sent with an admiring letter to Lady Caroline. She responded instead to his parents: 'for your son'. More poems followed and Caroline took to giving direct poetic advice, recommending that Bulwer should be his own man and not try to match famous writers such as Sir Walter Scott, giving a little list in which she included Lord Byron. The friendship ripened for a while into passionate love – at least on Bulwer's side. There was one Christmas of which he wrote: 'I did not make what is entitled "love" to her till I saw how acceptable it would be. In short, she appeared to feel for me even more than I felt for her.' There was a caveat: but 'she resisted what few women would have done'.[2] As he made clear later, his offer of a more physical passion was firmly rejected: theirs was 'a Platonic romance'. At least this romance was commemorated on both sides in their literary works: Bulwer featured in one of Caroline's novels as the Good Spirit, and in the words of Bulwer-Lytton's biographer, he 'tried to exorcise her ghost' in his novels and short stories on at least three occasions.[3]

From Caroline's point of view, however, it is made clear from the young Bulwer's reaction to her, 'the Daughter of Feeling' and the romance such as it was, that not all the magic was fled, despite illness. But illness was becoming a feature of her life: or was it something not strictly definable as illness – addiction to alcohol? This growing addiction was evident in her own papers. One letter to her physician Dr Goddard confesses: 'Sir, being unhappy today, I have drunk 1 whole bottle of wine which I bought for myself all at once without food.'[4] This weakness was readily confirmed by her enemies, including those within the Lamb family longing for the Separation. Then there was the laudanum which had been prescribed for her since childhood. Neither of these would have helped her to preserve her once delightful appearance.

On 13 November 1821, shortly after her mother's death, Caroline Lamb was thirty-six years old. Verdicts on her appearance varied. She was sometimes described as haggard, and indeed it took very little loss of weight for her tiny frame to appear skeletal. Yet she continued to exercise charm over those willing to concede it. The elfin look and the capacity to amuse, together with her true benevolence towards those less fortunate (or younger) than herself, remained to make her still something of the person that Byron had once admired with exasperated love.

Her own letters – including those to young Bulwer – are permeated by references to illness, feeling ill, recovering, falling ill again. 'This beautiful weather must I think cure any one,' she told Bulwer one day in May, 'and yet I feel as if nothing would for long do me good.' It was to her new friend the philosopher William Godwin however that she gave the most evocative description of her condition in her mid-thirties: 'I am like the wreck of a little boat, for I never come up to the sublime and beautiful – merely a gay little merry boat, which perhaps stranded itself at Vauxhall or London Bridge – or wounded without killing itself as a butterfly does in a tallow candle.'[5]

It was certainly true that, in the opinion of the world, this butterfly had wounded itself in a number of tallow candles, and one mighty flame in particular. But it was equally true that she could still enact a 'little merry boat'. When it came to the fortunes of her friends, Caroline continued to take on the task of helping them seriously. William Godwin was a prime example. Now in his sixties, he fascinated Caroline not only in his own right, but as the father of his 'very interesting and beautiful' daughter Mary whose mother Mary Wollstonecraft, the celebrated author of *A Vindication of the Rights of Woman*, had died at her birth, and herself was the author of *Frankenstein*, published in 1818. Caroline peppered him with invitations: 'My dear Sir. If you will call upon me as early as *12* [*sic*] or as late *10* [*sic*] in the Evening I am sure to be at home,' she wrote in June 1823, ending, 'If you think it worthwhile call upon me at 12 or 1 tomorrow. I will stay home on purpose to see you.'[6]

Lady Caroline also asked Godwin questions about suitable reading matter for Augustus: 'I am very anxious about my dear boy. I must speak to you about him.' She further introduced him to Edward Bulwer, 'a very young man and an enthusiast', at Bulwer's own request when he was at Cambridge. Her letters to him, apart from describing the beauties of Brocket and asking him to share them ('I will send my carriage to Barnet'), are full of questions: what does he think of Cobbett, for example? 'I think he writes better to my fancy than almost any one.' It was to Godwin that Caroline confessed that above all her need was for 'persons of high intellect'.[7]

But as Godwin fell into financial difficulties, Lady Caroline was among those who started to rally her friends to help him and William Lamb signed the appeal for public support. Caroline recommended writing, among others, to the Marquess of Lansdowne, Earl Fitzwilliam, Lord Dacre, her cousin the Duke of Devonshire, and Lord Grey. But she did not seek the credit: she specifically asked Godwin not to name her, but to write as from John Murray – perhaps she feared that the reputation of 'Calantha' might taint the appeal.[8]

Above all, whatever her tribulations, physical and emotional, including the continued problems of Augustus, Caroline Lamb continued to write books. This was indeed a period of extraordinary fertility of which any writer might be proud. *Gordon: A Tale: A Poetical Review of Don Juan*, another satire, was published in 1821, marking the appearance of Cantos I, IV and V of Byron's poem. Two serious novels followed. *Graham Hamilton* was published in the autumn of 1822 and *Ada Reis* a mere six months after that, in March 1823.

In *Gordon*, Caroline took it upon herself to tick Byron off for immorality in flamboyant style.[9] She had the satire, written in a parody of the style of *Don Juan*, privately printed and distributed it to friends, who were amused or otherwise by its diatribes. At first the great man is commended:

> Who can like him describe a dreadful scene?
> Who can like him bring forth a tender passion?
> Who can like him give an unsound machine
> Life, being, motion, harmony and fashion?

Before a note of warning emerges:

> Or who like him can paint the very worst
> Of sins in such a light, that even piety
> Can scarce preserve us from the dreadful thirst
> To sin *just so* ourselves? . . .

All the same, 'a noble strain, Worthy of Milton, or of Shakespeare even' is discerned.

Then 'A tall, thin man' emerges through 'a creaking door' and proceeds to denounce Byron's use of his great talent for 'Subjects too gross indeed to bear relation'. The tale rapidly involves the supernatural, 'a host of apparitions great and small', the tall, thin man himself being probably 'a real ghost'. The constant message of Byron's misuse of his talent in the interests of immorality is thumped home until 'those spectre groups' which make the narrator's blood run chill vanish in turn. So the narrator decides to quit her much-loved dwelling, where she had once resolved to live out her life:

> But soon I left the place where I resided,
> And so would you, if you had felt as I did.

As a privately printed effort, *Gordon* did not get official public attention beyond a sneer two years later in the *Morning Review*, hoping that it would be many moons before the author 're-commits himself to the press'.[10]

Graham Hamilton was an altogether more serious effort, attacking in effect the Whig Society in which Caroline Lamb had been raised.[11] At Caroline's request it was published anonymously by Henry Colburn (who had published *Glenarvon*) because William Lamb was anxious that the dreaded name of *Glenarvon* should not be conjured up in connection with the new book. William responded by correcting the proofs of the novel, 'as an occupation for his lonely hours'. It was a tradition he continued with Caroline's next book.[12]

Graham Hamilton himself is brought up in Scotland, heir to a rich uncle; he confides his story to a stranger, beginning with the confession: 'I possessed what is called the best of hearts – a dangerous possession, as it is generally accompanied by the strongest passions and the weakest judgement.' When he goes south, he falls into a platonic relationship with Lady Orville, a famous hostess: 'mistress of that mansion where all breathes delight and gaiety'. Lady Orville is a reckless gambler – shades of Georgiana Duchess of Devonshire, on whom the character is probably founded, attractive, kind and generous as she is. In the end Lady Orville loses everything, seized by the Sheriff's orders: 'beds, furniture, sofa, pictures, plate and everything'. She is found kneeling to heaven and praying for fortitude and resignation: the only course left to her. Worst of all her young son is taken away, in a terrible scene with the maid lamenting: 'what a desert our dwelling will be without this little cherub' and the boy himself piteously promising: 'Dear mother . . . sweet mamma, I will be so good always.'

It is Graham Hamilton who rescues Lady Orville by paying her debts, as a result of which he in turn goes to prison for debt. Hamilton is then rescued by his uncle and leaves for Europe, while Lady Orville discovers religion.

After that came *Ada Reis*, Caroline's most exciting book.[13] Her sister-in-law Emily dismissed it in a letter to her brother Frederick as 'a strange farrago', adding condescendingly, 'but you may think it is worth 15 shillings to satisfy your curiosity'. In spite of this predictable reaction, *Ada Reis* does in fact combine remarkable research and a bold narrative to great effect. Caroline had worked on it for several years: she had written roguishly to her mother in her last months, telling her of a 'strange wild story' called *Ada Reis* 'written, they say, by an American' and offering to send her a rough printed proof if one was available.[14] She tried Thomas Malthus, the celebrated scholar of demography, whom she had once met at a ball, for help and was turned down.

Ugo Foscolo had also been approached. 'May I ask a favour?' she had begun. 'I have written a tale, not a novel, it is full of mistakes, and I feel perhaps that it is no good . . . Do me this favour, let your Maid-of-all-work read it to you and tell me frankly "I like or do not like this or that".' She flattered Foscolo by telling him that he was the only person apart from 'Mr. Lamb' to have the 'sound judgement and admirable simplicity' to tell the truth.[15]

Ada Reis – the word Ada means a male chief, not to be confused with the female forename – is 'the Don Juan of his day' and there are undoubtedly Byronic echoes here, as well as something of Caroline's adventurer friend Michael Bruce. Caroline dedicated it to Lydia White, who presided over a literary salon of the sort she now increasingly enjoyed. Significantly, Lydia White was a woman who had not allowed appalling health to banish her from London Society: her appearance was summed up as 'rouged and dying' by Maria Edgeworth. Caroline in her dedication referred to her as one not 'paying undue reference to the world'. She described the Moral of the tale: 'he, who remains amidst the busy scenes of life, himself without employment, is in constant danger of becoming the prey of wicked feelings and corrupt passions, for as use preserves iron from rust, so labour and exertion purify and invigorate the soul'. In short this was to be another assault on the idle aristocratic way of life in which she had been nurtured, compared to the values of hard work. The basic story concerns a deal done by Ada Reis with the Spirit of Evil and how it goes wrong, told in highly colourful dramatic turns, with wild South American scenes. She offered it to John Murray, referring to it encouragingly: 'It is not personal, it will make no row,' adding, 'It need never be known to be mine.' Under the circumstances, 'pray therefore fear not to let it have your name'.[16]

Caroline may not have seen *Ada Reis* as personal, but the character of Fiormonda, daughter of Reis, a mixture of a lovely, gentle child and a wildly bad-tempered termagant, clearly owes much to the author. It is to Fiormonda that the words which might have been the motto of Lady Caroline Lamb were applied: 'How vain are the commands of a despot, and of what avail is force against the free spirit.'[17] The central character Ada Reis, with his clear auburn hair hanging in curls on his white neck, is from the first a mixture of good and evil; from humble slave origins, he is dominated by a prophecy: 'Continue thy course: a monarch's crown awaits thee, in a land where diamonds and emeralds shall be strewn under thy feet.' The land concerned is South America, where Ada Reis settles first as an agent of the Spanish government, then discovers treasure and finds himself in Lima, 'the city of kings'.

As Fiormonda grows up, developing beyond an innocent passion for pages – shades of Caroline herself – a series of dark characters emerge, and Ada Reis's fortunes decline horribly. The story finishes with Ada Reis in the Cave Bocca Inferno, where Kabkarra, the Spirit of Evil, appears as a monstrous spider.

'Restore me to my child Fiormonda and I will be your slave,' cries Ada Reis. 'You are my slave already,' is the grim reply. A tour follows of what is in effect Hell, producing some insights into the position of women and men in the infernal regions – and incidentally into Caroline Lamb's own views. Reis is surprised that there are so many more men than women. Kabkarra explains to him that 'women are punished on earth for their offences', although a clamour reveals that there are indeed certain females present below who are suffering a humiliating punishment. 'The former ladies', says Kabkarra, smiling, 'are here the servants; their merciless caprices, their unreasonable expectations, their vanity, their meanness, are all returned upon themselves.'

The Conclusion to the book describes two mountains in Guatemala where the native Indians imagine that a Good and an Evil spirit dwell within these heights. The Good Spirit (founded on Caroline's admirer Bulwer) is said to inhabit 'the verdant mountains, where spring ever reigns; and the Evil spirit to dwell in the volcano, from whence it rushes forth in flame and desolation. Thus ends the story of Ada Reis! . . . Look then, into your own heart; repent, and pray; beware the fate of Ada Reis, for however seductive the paths of pleasure . . . remember that, step by step they lead to the gate of the burning vault.' Over that is written a quotation from Dante's *Inferno*: 'Abandon every hope, you who enter here.' Only Fiormonda can be said to have a happy ending of sorts: she ends up as a Christian penitent.

The reception of *Ada Reis* was varied, many papers taking the 'farrago' line of Emily Cowper, others being more benevolent even if a note of condescension was generally to be detected. Caroline could take comfort from the songs in the novel to which her friend Isaac Nathan had composed music and printed it. Caroline responded that she meant to send his wife *Ada Reis*, meanwhile 'Tell my God-daughter to love me.' It was a measure of their continuing friendship, so much valued by Caroline, that when Emily Nathan died in childbirth in January 1824, Nathan asked Caroline to 'versify' some Hebrew lines, which she duly did, beginning:

> As the flower early gathered, while fresh in its bloom
> So was she whom I mourn for sent young to the tomb
> In the pain of her travail, the prime of her youth
> Whilst the memory survives of her sweetness and truth[18]

*

There was another side to Caroline's life to this point, beyond her stimulating literary life on the one hand and the ill health which dogged her on the other. This was the ominous thunder-cloud over her head in the shape of the Lamb family's continuing determination to secure a legal Separation for William. Rumours of this Separation had now been rife for many years since Byron enquired of Lady Melbourne if it was true about '*les agneaux*', as he chose to call them, being parted. At which point Lady M. replied that it was 'a wicked scandal'.[19]

The sticking point was always William himself. As Caroline's health declined, with drink or drugs both likely to feature in any attack on her character, so the need for care, including nurses trained in the handling of the mad (in the all-embracing nineteenth-century term), increased. William too began to weaken. In late 1822 he exploded to Emily about his unhappiness, and talked of seeing Caroline as she really was, as a result of her tempers. The most sinister words were those when he stressed 'the injury' she had been to him. He meant political injury.[20]

Before negotiations began, there was an event which can only have increased the state of melancholy into which Caroline was sinking, despite her bold efforts at striking a literary course on the one hand and reaching out from Brocket on the other. On 19 April 1824 Lord Byron died in Greece from a violent fever, hastened on to death by fierce medical blood-letting. He was thirty-six.

Byron's body was brought back to England and escorted by Hobhouse, who met the ship at London Docks. He had the tragic task of supervising the transferral of the body from a Greek cask to a properly dignified lead coffin. It lay in state in a room in Westminster hired by Hobhouse before a procession, watched by huge crowds, set out through London. Thereafter the cortège consisted of the undertakers and the hearse.

The destination was the poet's family vault at Hucknall Tork-ard in Nottinghamshire: a three-day journey. It was while the cortège was in Hertfordshire that the extraordinary encounter took place which might argue for some supernatural bond between Byron and Lady Caroline Lamb. Indeed, she herself told Thomas Medwin later, while Byron was still alive, that she suddenly fancied she saw him in the middle of the night. She had jumped out of bed screaming, to be confronted by a speechless figure: 'he looked horrible and ground his teeth at me'. At the time she was convinced that she herself was going to die and later never dared check to see if it was the actual date of Byron's death.[21]

The real news was actually told to her some time later, in her own words to Medwin, as she was 'laughing at Brocket Hall'.

She was in her open carriage having her first outing after a period of illness, escorted by William Lamb on horseback. William met the cortège at the turnpike and asked out of curiosity whose hearse it was. The unbelievable, chilling answer threw Caroline into despair. She wrote simply to John Murray on 13 July: 'Lord Byron's Hearse came by our gates Yesterday. You may judge what I felt . . .'. To Hart, on the other hand, she allowed herself to be more emotional: 'My very Dearest Kindest Cousin . . . My heart is in mourning at hearing of Lord Byron's death . . .'.[22]

If Caroline's mind went back to her final meeting with Byron, this had been in 1814 in Albany. Or so Caroline would tell Thomas Medwin later: 'the last time we parted for ever, as he pressed his lips on mine . . . he said "poor Caro, if every one hates me, you, I see will never change – No, not with ill usage!"'. To which Caroline replied: 'yes, I *am* changed, & shall come near you no more'. This was a dignified memory to cling to; she spoilt it by adding that Byron had told her various unsavoury things about his past.[23]

But there was worse, much worse, to come. Thomas Medwin now published that demonic poem by Byron in response to her visit to his apartment and her admonishment to remember her. 'Remember thee!' had echoed Byron, proceeding to the terrible line which summed up Lady Caroline Lamb so conveniently to her enemies: 'Thou false to him, thou fiend to me.' As when Lord Melbourne had told Caroline contemptuously that Byron would not receive her if she ran to him, this was the kind of stab which reached deep.

On the domestic front, life was no happier. Negotiations began at last for the famous Separation. Not surprisingly, relations between the Lambs and the Ponsonbys were increasingly hostile. Caroline's brothers George and Fred negotiated on her behalf. Following his wounding at Waterloo, when Caroline had succoured him, Fred had gone on half-pay in 1820, but returned to the army in 1824 as Field Officer in the Ionian Islands; he would be made Lieutenant-Governor of Malta the next year, as has been noted. Emily Cowper took a part, boasting at one point: 'I have bullied the bully.' Cousin Hart was, according to his wont where his beloved Caroline was concerned, as helpful as he could be. In the end Hart and Lord Cowper, Emily's husband, reached an agreement of a payment of £2,500 now, £3,000 thereafter, together with £2,000 for setting out. 'It is certainly a great deal more than she deserves,' sniffed Emily. Hart's reaction was more important: he talked of the liberality and handsomeness of the arrangement.[24]*

Caroline was given a London house at 39 Conduit Street which had the advantage that it was close to her publisher John Murray, in Albemarle Street. At least in London she continued her friendship with the chivalrous Duke of Wellington, in whose company she could be perhaps the gay merry little boat which had amused him originally. One characteristic encounter occurred not in London but in Brighton. The Duke reported to Mrs Arbuthnot that Caroline had jumped out of her carriage to come to him on the East Cliffe 'mad as a March hare' and 'did not wait to have the Steps let down!'. Immediately Caroline gave the Duke news of her latest book – *Ada Reis* – with the tantalising comment: 'She says it was doubtful whether it was written by Lord Byron or Thomas Hope!' The reference was to a celebrated Anglo-Dutch interior decorator, who had recently written a novel *Anastasius: Or, Memoirs of a Greek* but was derided by Byron as

---

* In modern values, £100 in 1825 is just under £9,000. Thus Caroline Lamb was being paid an annual allowance of very roughly a quarter of a million pounds. Her 'setting out' payment was around £175,000.

'the furniture man'. The Duke in turn promised to pass the book on to Mrs Arbuthnot.[25]

There was a sadder moment when the Duke wrote in August 1824, evidently in reply to information from Mrs Arbuthnot herself, 'I had never heard of Calantha's drinking! How very shocking.' Although it does indicate that Caroline was still capable of a social life – with the Duke – without overdoing the drink. Fortunately, the next day Wellington encountered Lady Caroline, who followed him into his Yard, where he was on his way to Panshanger, the house and surrounding park of the Cowpers, not far from Brocket. 'She looked as well if not better [than] when I saw her last.' Caroline then told the Duke that she had been very unwell at Brocket, and therefore could not visit him at Panshanger.[26]

A bulletin from the Duke towards the end of the year found 'Calantha' being outraged with Captain Medwin 'for what do you think? Because he says that Lord Byron was not in love with her, and she swears that she can prove that he was; and will publish his letters!' The Duke reflected: 'Delightful Society! These people of Genius make!!'[27] On this occasion, for all his kindness, the Duke did show a certain lack of human sympathy as to what Byron might have meant to 'Calantha' and how deeply Medwin's words had wounded her in consequence.

Caroline did in fact protest to Medwin at great length in November 1824 after the publication of his book *Conversations with Lord Byron*. Her anguished letter tells the story from the beginning from Caroline's point of view. How she was not 'a woman of the world': 'had I been one of that sort, why should he have devoted entire months almost entirely to my society'. Then: 'he broke my heart. Still I love him – witness the agony I experienced at his death & the tears your book has cost me.' Her constant need was once more to prove Byron's love for her.[28]

For the next few years, Caroline's health went on a sad downward journey with occasional respites. There were still incidents in her life when Society was reminded of the risky character of 'Calantha'. One Wilmington Fleming, an aspiring poet, attempted some kind of blackmail, despite or because of Lady Caroline

Lamb's well-meant attempts to draw him into her literary circle – even if that literary circle was fast becoming a fantasy, in view of her health, and what was generally taken by the world to be her madness, as described by Dr Goddard. When Harriette Wilson published her *Memoirs*, Fleming stepped forward with an edited version of Caroline's *Journals*, predictably casting aspersions on Byron and others. It is not quite clear how the whole squalid business ended: Lady Caroline's own version was that her brother's solicitor had paid up for the return of the *Journals*.[29]

Meantime the publication of Harriette Wilson's *Memoirs* took place. This was the work to which the Duke of Wellington had famously responded 'Publish and be damned' when Harriette made an attempt to blackmail him. It included a list of her celebrated lovers, not only the Duke himself but the Marquess of Worcester, Beau Brummell and the Duke of Leinster. Hardly surprisingly, the book ran through thirty editions in one year.

It also involved Lady Caroline Lamb in public obloquy again. Harriette Wilson chose to respond to public criticism of her morals, as revealed in her book, with a protest that Caroline, who had behaved far more badly, had never been insulted. 'Now I beg to ask the editor of the *New Times*, what can be more immoral than Lady Caroline Lamb, a wife and mother, publishing her own desperate love letters to Lord Byron. Yet no editor ever took her to task since her friends were on the spot.' Caroline's response to this was witty, if not exactly dignified. She wrote a poem pointing out that Harriette had been paid for her services (and should therefore have shut up) whereas she had not.[30]

> Harriette Wilson, shall I tell thee where
> Besides my being *cleverer,*
> We differ? Thou were hired to hold thy tongue
> Thou hast no right to do thy lovers wrong . . .

As for her own revelations:

> Why should I hide men's follies, whilst my own
> Blaze like the gas along this talking town

The poem ended flippantly:

> In the meantime – we Lambs are seldom civil
> I wish thy book – *not thee* – at the Devil.

It was politics which brought to an end the situation in which the Lambs were separated, but somehow not disconnected. Augustus – now virtually grown up – was only one of the many links between them, which it seemed would never be altogether broken. Caroline continued to express herself from time to time in agonising poems such as this, in reply to William's theoretical question, asking her what she wanted:

> O grant it – leave me what I have
> Leave me to rest upon my bed
> With broken heart and weary head.
>
> No stormy passions now arise,
> Nor tears relieve these suffering eyes.[31]

In April 1827 William was made Chief Secretary to the Lord Lieutenant of Ireland. The Lamb family were understandably gleeful. 'Now he has everything open to him', wrote Emily, with Caroline 'no longer a millstone'.[32] Lamb was in fact a sensible political choice at this tricky moment in Irish history when the prospect of Catholic Emancipation was being dangled, now withdrawn without resolution, given William Lamb's own tolerance of Catholics and Protestants, believing himself friendly to both religions.

The Secretaryship involved residence in Dublin. Crucially from Caroline's point of view, William took Augustus with him. This was Caroline's wish: it was much better for him than being with women and children where he learnt nothing 'and grows silly'.[33] The boy was now nearly twenty. He could read and write – although some of his letters show signs of being helped on by others, not surprisingly given that he would henceforth have to correspond with his mother across the Irish Sea. He continued to have fits, which were kept in control by doctors; but he was amiable. It is to William's credit that he does not seem to have objected to the plan on this, his first official posting (at the age of forty-eight). This wish to please Caroline and his own tolerant nature combined to make him fall in with the proposal. Caroline's chief desire was that her beloved boy should have some kind of normalcy in his life – and although probably a pipe dream, it was in theory a better alternative than lurking in the country with an increasingly invalid mother.

It is true that this unselfish view sometimes degenerated into sheer misery, just as her resignation to the Separation would turn into explosion against William's family. She would wail about Augustus: 'remember me to my own sweet kind boy, no one wrote to me on his birthday'. The little boat, for all its periodic gaiety, was at long last in danger of being stranded permanently.

CHAPTER TWELVE

Melancholy

*'How unfortunate and melancholy that
you should be so ill now'*

William Lamb, 1828

WILLIAM LAMB WROTE to Caroline, from Ireland where he was now Chief Secretary, in early January 1828. The letter began: 'My heart is broken that I cannot come over directly.' He went on: 'How unfortunate and melancholy that you should be so ill now, or that it should be at a time when I, who have had so many years of idleness, am so fixed and chained by circumstances.'[1] The letter was in fact in the form of an apology for not immediately abandoning his post in view of Caroline's rapidly declining health.

The declaration of heartbreak was doubtless true as he penned the letter. This was a time of huge official responsibilities in Ireland, and a testing time for him personally in his first real political appointment. He could not travel, he should not travel, and yet surely he wanted to travel. He truly loved his wife – his separated wife – but he had accepted a distant political post at a time when it must have been clear that she did not have many more years to live. If William did not remember the extraordinary tolerance he had shown towards Caroline at critical moments in the past – and why should he not? – there were plenty of family members to remind him about it. These remaining months in Caroline's life would thus be spent outside William's radius for the first time since they met, virtually as children, at any rate as young teenagers in the environs of the Devonshire Set.[2]

The fact was that William Lamb was beginning to move away for the first time from under the spell that Caroline had cast upon him for so long. In the autumn of 1827, shortly after his arrival in Dublin, he began to conduct the first known love affair since his marriage to Caroline in 1805. This persistent fidelity, in view of his wife's own flagrant infidelity, comes as a surprise and yet any deviation would surely have been chronicled, if not by Caroline, by the exulting Emily and other family members, including his powerful mother.

Elizabeth Brandon, born into the Irish family of La Touche, had married an elder debt-ridden cousin who was also a clergyman and a peer, Lord Brandon. Undoubtedly she fell passionately in love with William, and he in return had the pleasure of securing preferment for her family via his official position. Rather as Byron had been reminded of Caroline by Teresa Guiccoli, William told his sister-in-law, George's wife, that Elizabeth Brandon was 'very like in her ways' to Caroline.[3] This was the life's experience that neither Byron nor William could forget.

Back in England, the life of Lady Caroline, herself a disgraced and separated wife, had certainly been lacking in excitement by her own standards during the two years that passed before William's departure. In vain she regretted pleasures gone by in a piteous letter to Lady Morgan: 'I would give all I possessed on earth to be again what I once was, and I would now be obedient and gentle.'

There was a Brocket Festival, organised by Isaac Nathan in June 1825, ironically under the circumstances, to mark her wedding day twenty years earlier.

> Now the ballroom opens and how splendid the scene
> Where Caroline sits, of the revels the Queen

But the truth was that the festival was suffused with sadness, the knowledge that 'the Queen' was no longer actually on the throne.[4]

Caroline made a sortie to Paris in August 1825, heavily encouraged by Emily Cowper who went to Dover and saw her off, with the uncharitable hope that she would be so sick that the bad crossing would deter her from returning too soon.[5]

Once at Calais, Caroline made a point of sending for her horses – 'my Mare, the young horse, Tom Croft [the groom]' – in a pleading letter to William: 'my Health depends upon riding & the expense of keeping these Horses is less than the money I am obliged to pay for hiring even a gig'. Then the tone of the letter changed into that of an unhappy, even desperate exile. How could William have let her be ousted in such a barbarous fashion: 'The Devil take the deed that took my Willy from me . . .'.[6]

In fact William could not be accused of lack of care for her in these years before his departure for Ireland, to the extent that Emily Cowper protested: 'William goes to see *her* too much,' laughing with Caroline in the old way until a quarrel might end the encounter. Later, he still showed his continuous devotion by riding down to see her at Brocket 'in the Morn'. Once again Emily was not best pleased. 'I think it *bad* her being there.' The two decisions taken – to agree to a legal Separation, and to accept a distant political office – would seem to indicate a new, more callous William Lamb; and yet events indicated that the previous indulgent – or indolent – spouse could not be altogether eliminated.[7]

Caroline was back from the French expedition by October, when she signed the Deed which allowed her to live in London. Contradictorily, Dr Goddard was persuaded by Emily Lamb to diagnose Lady Caroline as 'insane'. Evidently the fits of 'madness' continued, as they had persisted all her life since childhood, when she had laughingly diagnosed herself as 'mad/That's bad' and more prophetically, 'sad/That's bad'.[8] And yet at other times she continued to enjoy what seemed to her a normal life.

Caroline's own residence in England wavered between addresses after the Separation. The idea of leaving Brocket upset her deeply. Her friend Isaac Nathan revealed a poem which Caroline was said to have read aloud sitting amid the birds under the tree where the young Queen Elizabeth I had once sat:

> Come sing upon your favourite tree
> Once more your sweetest songs to me
> An exile from these scenes I go
> Whither I neither care nor know[9]

Brocket was the place she loved most on earth. And yet there was an ever-present danger there: there was talk of restraint and straitjackets. She might be put away with nurses and – in her terms – forgotten.

For the next few years Caroline's life tottered forward, including periods when she was allowed to go to her beloved Brocket. There were nurses, doctors and conferences (to which Caroline was not party) as to whether she should not be confined in some form of 'Bedlam', in the contemporary phrase. While at Panshanger the Duke of Wellington was told of one occasion when she tore up the doctor's report and generally behaved hysterically. Yet he was careful to add that the next time he saw the woman he called Calantha, she was perfectly quiet.[10]

Caroline herself gave an optimistic view of life at Brocket to Bulwer in August 1826 as being: 'happy, Healthy *quiet* contented I get up at ½ past 4 and ride about with Haggard [the groundkeeper] and see Harvest men at work in this pretty confined green Country – read a few old Books, see no one hear from no one and occasionally play at Chess with Dr. Goddard . . .'. She went on to point out that she had drawn her Good Spirit in *Ada Reis* from him and hoped Bulwer had not turned into a bad one. Which meant she wanted a letter. But Caroline's brief romantic – but platonic – fling with Bulwer was over. He remained adoringly in Caroline's circle and it was in fact Caroline who introduced him to his future wife.

Caroline still had some kind of London life. There was an occasion at the Mayfair literary salon of Miss Anne Isabella Spence (to which Caroline was happy to be invited for her 'litt'ry' abilities) when one observer noted: 'Lady Caroline Lamb was accompanied by a young and singularly beautiful lady, whose form and features were then as near perfection, as art, or even fancy could conceive them.'[11] This was Rosina Wheeler.

Rosina's friendship with Caroline had taken a familiar course of eccentric generosity. At one point Caroline promised her a dog, and on presenting it sensed 'dismay' in Rosina's countenance which she attributed to Rosina not liking the dog, a poodle. 'Oh, I see you don't like Miss Lamb [as she called the puppy] so I'll get you another from Duncannon.' She added: 'Or you shall have one of those pretty spaniels of the Duke of Devonshire's that you admire so much.' Hastily, Rosina assured Lady Caroline that she liked the dog very much. Caroline introduced Bulwer to Rosina and they married in August 1827.[12]

The friendship with William Godwin, so much valued as 'a person of high intellect', in her own words 'the type she needed around her', continued. And Godwin received her confidences, as when she exclaimed in a letter commending his works which she was attempting to introduce to her family circle, with better luck with the men than the women.[13]

It was to Godwin that she confided her admirable new philosophy as her life visibly declined. 'After all, what is the use of anything here below but to be enlightened, and to try to make others happy?' She added: 'From this day I will endeavour to conquer all my violence, all my passions . . . Oh, that I might, with the feelings I yet possess, without one vain, one ambitious motive, at least feel that I was in the way of truth, and that I was of use to others.'[14]

The Ponsonby family of brothers continued to support their sister. There was some kind of social life in the country as well as London: for example, Caroline dined with Lord and Lady Salisbury at neighbouring Hatfield and met her kindly patron the Duke of Wellington, whom she found to be looking 'uncommonly well'. Augustus, her beloved boy, remained her preoccupation and was the subject of long letters of maternal advice, ranging from taking care with cricket balls to keeping a hat on in hot weather. Together with the adopted Susan Churchill, she could also share with him her delight in Brocket itself: in July 1827 Susan wrote to Augustus in Dublin, 'Brocket is looking beautiful and all the flowers are in bloom.' The lake had recently been cleaned out; she reported how 'Lady Caroline often goes upon it in the boat.'[15]

Augustus's twentieth birthday in August was marked by a letter from Caroline to Dublin, incidentally making it clear that William was doing his best to keep in contact despite his decision to accept the post of Chief Secretary. 'My dearest own boy – how very good your father has been about writing – Susan wishes very much for a letter – she sends the only sovereign she has got to buy you a birthday present and I four for the same purpose.'[16] Augustus for his part replied in terms which, although desperately polite, made it quite clear that like many other men with a bookish mother his interest in literature did not equal Caroline's. In huge, clear and beautiful handwriting he thanked his 'dear Mother' for her 'kind letter' but went on to say: 'I am much obliged to you for offering to send me some books here which I can read but as Mr. Lamb has several books here which I can read I think it is not necessary to send any so great a distance.' Caroline would have been better pleased by the letter's ending: 'I am in very good health at present and the attacks are not near so frequent as they have been lately, a good deal lighter than usual.'

The fight over Byron's legacy – his memories as in his *Journals*, read, remembered or imagined – continued and was a great deal less pleasant as an influence in her life than her maternal preoccupation. Caroline's position was an awkward one. She had been allowed by John Murray to read Byron's *Journals* before he destroyed them according to instructions from the poet; she had suffered from the denial of 'that moment', denial that there had been any real love on his part, which never failed, understandably, to inflict a terrible wound on her heart. Medwin's testimony in his *Conversations* remained the most painful: the admission by the poet that she had gained 'an ascendancy' over him that was not easily shaken off had to be balanced against his crude (and contradictory) statement that Caroline had 'scarcely any personal attractions to commend her'.[17]

Caroline wrote to her sympathetic friend William Godwin: 'Have you read Medwin's Book – the part respecting me gives me much pain – this is strange – why need I care – I do however – but what matters all this to you –' and Caroline reverted to hoping Godwin would come next week to Brocket.[18]

The downward slant of her physical health, as opposed to her mental health, continued. The dropsy which was diagnosed, probably as a result of the laudanum which she had taken – or been given – for so long, combined with the alcohol which she had not taken for quite so long, would now be known as oedema, or swelling due to fluid retention, eventually leading to heart failure. As a result the adorable boy-girl who had enchanted Byron had vanished; Caroline was now sadly swollen by her disease. It had a long medical history.*

The treatments were all extremely unpleasant: 'blue pills, squills, and sweet spirits of nitre, with an infusion of cascarilla bark' was how Caroline described them; what little strength she had was diminished by a process of blood-letting or tapping, which left her feeling 'deadly cold and sick'.[19] Caroline Lamb endured it all, but that stage could not last forever.

Finally, in October 1827, it was thought right to bring her back to London, to Melbourne House, the site of those very different scenes at the start of her marriage over twenty years earlier. Dr Goddard, in charge of Caroline with the aid of nurses, informed William at his wife's request, admitting that he had wished to do so some time before. He gave him Caroline's medical details, adding: 'Her conduct has been very amicable, indeed her behaviour of late has altered very much in every respect the better – she appears she cannot ultimately recover but with feelings of perfect resignation says she does not mind to die.'[20]

---

* Dropsy is referred to in the Bible (Luke 14:1–6) when Jesus healed a man of dropsy at the house of the chief Pharisee despite it being the Sabbath Day; Jesus asked pointedly which of them would not have saved an ass or an ox fallen into a pit on the Sabbath.

It was at this point that William, having received the joint summon of his wife and her doctor, had declared himself unable to travel, in his own words in the letter quoted earlier, his 'heart . . . broken'. A few days later, on 21 January 1828, a change of government took place when the Prime Minister, Lord Goderich, who had attempted unsuccessfully to keep the Canningite government together after the latter's death, resigned. The Duke of Wellington marched in. Politically, not personally, William Lamb now needed to be in London. He set off, accompanied by Augustus. The journey from Holyhead was horrendous: a heavy gale of wind against them meant that it took more than fifteen hours.

Father and son reached Melbourne House in time to see Caroline in her last fragile stages of life. It was in keeping with her character, the true courage that lay beneath the tempest and the frivolity, that in her husband's words, 'She is dying, dying rapidly, and that with a perfect knowledge of it and the greatest composure.' Afterwards, Caroline's brother Willy Ponsonby confirmed that William's visit had given her much comfort: 'from the beginning she had no expectation of recovery and only wanted to live long enough to see Mr. Lamb again. She *did* and was able to converse with him.' Ponsonby added, touchingly: Caroline was able to 'enjoy his society' before she died – as she had done all her life.[21]

When the moment of death arrived on Sunday night at about nine o'clock, it so happened that William was not actually there. It did not matter. She was content. The dying woman 'only fetched one sigh and she was gone'. Caroline Lamb was forty-two years old.

For William Lamb a unique, sparkling light had gone out in the world. In his own words: 'I felt . . . a sort of impossibility of believing that I should never see her countenance or hear her voice again, and a sort of sense of desolation, solitude and carelessness about everything when I forced myself to remember that she really was gone.'[22]

The husband of Caroline Lamb never married again.

Remember Thee!

'Remember thee! Remember thee!'

Lord Byron

L ADY CAROLINE LAMB was taken to lie alongside the children she had lost at birth in St Etheldreda's Church, Hatfield; her body in its hearse conveyed from London as once upon a time had that of Byron, so fatefully encountered. She was buried on 7 February 1828.

A few years later, when Augustus died, he too was taken to lie beside her. One day William Lamb would join them. Before that a whole new existence awaited him.

Symbolically, William Lamb began his new life after Caroline with a new name: his father died five months after his wife's death and at the age of forty-nine he became the 2nd Viscount Melbourne. It is a small but important point that Lady Caroline Lamb was never actually Lady Melbourne.*

William on the other hand, under the name of Melbourne, became Prime Minister briefly in 1834, and then for a significant

---

* Thus she should not be indexed or referred to as Caroline Lamb Lady Melbourne since this swallows her up into a life of which she was never actually part.

six years from 1835 to 1841, a period which included the accession of Victoria to the throne at the age of eighteen. To the delight of both parties, the middle-aged, still handsome Prime Minister was able to act as the charming new Queen's mentor. The young Victoria showed herself intrigued by her Prime Minister's private history.

From the information she derived, Victoria was inclined to refer to 'that shocking wife of his'.[1] Emily Cowper, by now a widow, gave a more considered judgement: Caroline was 'very clever and full of talent, but so wild and so frightfully passionate, really not quite right . . . and yet she had something about her which made people forgive her'. Caroline's critical cousins were beginning to melt towards her in their recollections. Harryo Granville, for example, was deeply moved by an account of Caroline's 'patience and resignation' on her deathbed, and inclined to think her education – did she mean the blatant immorality of her mother? – to blame for her faults.[2]

The young Queen came from a different generation (she was nearly thirty-five years younger than Caroline). She made up her own mind. Victoria decided to her own satisfaction that Caroline had 'quite embittered his [Melbourne's] life which it should have been her pride to study to render a happy one'. In those early days of her reign, perhaps Victoria felt that this was her task. All this was in effect Melbourne's public life.[3]

His private life was to be very different. In terms of the young, William behaved notably well, as an essentially kind man was likely to do. Apart from tending to Augustus, he looked after the young Susan Churchill, whom Caroline had taken on after her mother's death, and sent her to school in Switzerland as a teenager. It was there that Susan found her husband Aimé Cuénard, son of the minister of a parish on the shores of Lake Geneva. Aimé himself became a banker, which was perhaps just as well, since the happy pair went on to have ten children in seventeen years, the eldest two being appropriately christened Caroline and William.[4]

One might note in complete contrast another successful story in the afterlife of Caroline Lamb's circle. Isaac Nathan eventually emigrated to Australia, where he became incidentally fascinated by the native Aboriginal airs. He would compose what has been termed 'the first Australian opera', *Don John of Austria*, first performed in Sydney in 1847.[5] These two, the young girl and the aspiring composer, stand for Caroline's benevolence, both maternal and creative.

Returning to William, the rest of his story was not quite so admirable. The first case of adultery actually brought against him was while he was in Ireland, after his wife's death, when Lady Brandon was named; payment was made and it was settled. By one of those strange turns of history, his agent in the matter was that high-spirited Byronic adventurer Michael Bruce, once featured as Caroline's admirer, if not more. William's *amitié amoureuse* with a married woman, the Hon. Mrs George Norton (Caroline), brought further legal trouble of a more flagrant sort. Efforts were made to marry him off, including to Emily Eden, the intelligent spinster sister of the Viceroy of India, Lord Auckland. As we have seen, all these efforts were made in vain. William Lamb Lord Melbourne would die a widower.

Augustus, the only child of William and Caroline, her 'dearest boy', died peacefully at the age of twenty-nine in 1836. Melbourne's heir was now his brother Frederick Lamb, who became the 3rd Viscount Melbourne at his death in 1848; but Frederick died childless, as did George Lamb, and so the line petered out and the title became extinct.

Thus Caroline left no descendants. Her legacy is different. The story of Lady Caroline Lamb exemplifies the captivity of a young female in the early nineteenth century before any kind of amelioration by reform had taken place. Caroline's notable addiction to dressing up as a boy – as a page – does not represent a sincere wish for transition to the masculine gender (as it might in the twenty-first century) so much as a wish for the freedom such a state conveyed. It was after all her spirited adventure posing as a page which gained her the wifely pleasure of hearing William Lamb's first Parliamentary speech: like her rather less admirable stalkings of Lord Byron after their parting, the dressing-up was done with a purpose, one she believed could not be achieved by a female.

Above all, she stands for the kind of independent woman at the beginning of the age of campaigning for female rights whose life and prospects would have been much improved by them. It might be thought that her life does not deserve complaint: aristocratic birth and the advantages it brought, prosperity compared to most, marriage for love, and when further love came it came in the shape of a genius. But there is an alternative Caroline hidden beneath this surface: an intelligent, original, questioning woman, seizing her limited opportunities to help, benefit and educate the less fortunate.

One can only imagine how she might have been if she lived in the age of the Suffragettes, or indeed when university education began to trickle down to the female sex. Her zest for electioneering on behalf of George Lamb signified one side of her nature; her reflective remarks to Lady Holland about men, the Lords of Creation, being just as much women's slaves and unable to do without them, portrayed the other.[6]

Caroline Lamb would still have been the little volcano, wilful, wayward, wild; but there might have been more to show for the wilfulness, the waywardness and the wildness than the scorn of historians, sandwiched as she is between the two great men in her life, Melbourne and Byron, one of whom gave his own all too memorable verdict: 'Thou false to him, thou fiend to me.' It must also be remembered that when Byron called her a little volcano that poured lava through her veins he added, 'and yet I cannot wish it a bit colder'.[7]

Her haunting wish to find a personal mission certainly concentrated far too long on a poet who, for all his genius, was no more free from human failings than she was. Her extraordinary courage, admirable in itself, helped her into a relationship with Lord Byron, but also enabled her to defame it for too long afterwards with outrageous behaviour provoked by deep disappointment.

It is perhaps fairer to end on the judgement of two very dissimilar people who were both in their own ways admirers of Caroline Lamb. First, Isaac Nathan, coming from a totally different background, in his *Fugitive Pieces and Reminiscences* praised her for 'an open frankness, which endeared her to all her high circle of acquaintance', before making the important contemporary point: 'openness of manner in the female character often leads to a misconception of nature', cloaking the serious real person. Secondly, Sydney Morgan was a highly intelligent woman with no family axe to grind who loved her. In an affectionate tribute, Lady Morgan emphasised the combination of impulse and 'a powerful imagination' which made Lady Caroline Lamb what she was: 'One of her great charms was the rapid transition of manner which changed to its theme.'[8] The modern phrase might be 'a lack of self-discipline' – but then had Caroline Lamb ever been instructed about discipline? As a female member of an apparently privileged class, she was expected to follow the rules obediently and even joyfully. And this Caroline Lamb never did. She found her joys elsewhere: romantic love which she refused to disguise, books based on her own story of which she refused to be ashamed.

Finally, where Caroline is concerned, it is tempting to quote Milton in *Paradise Lost*:

> What though the field be lost?
> All is not lost, th'unconquerable will . . .
> And courage never to submit or yield[9]

Lady Caroline Lamb showed the 'courage never to submit or yield', in the words of the poet. This is in fact Milton describing Lucifer's attitude after his fall – and there were indeed those in her own time and later who would think the comparison of Caroline to Lucifer not too far-fetched. But Caroline Lamb was neither Lucifer nor an angel.

She should be remembered for what she was: a Free Spirit.

A.F., Feast of St Antony, 2022

REFERENCES

CHAPTER ONE:
LOVELY AND LIVELY
1 cit. Douglass, p. 5
2 Journal of Lady Spencer, 1785, Devonshire MSS, 5th Duke's Group, f. 2014.155
3 Mitchell, *Whig World*, p. 47; Clarke, p. 37
4 Foreman, p. 98; Mitchell, *Whig World*, p. 25
5 Askwith, p. 25 *et seq.*; Douglass, p. 156
6 Stourton, p. 87
7 L.C.L., *Letters*, pp. 10–11
8 Ibid., p. 10
9 Hist. Parlt., G.E.C., Vol. I, pp. 10–11; Foreman, p. 87
10 Spencer, p. xv; Foreman, p. 4
11 Brown, p. 55
12 Byron, *L. & J.*, Vol. 7, p. 169; Gleeson, p. 7
13 Kelly, p. 168
14 Mitchell, *Whig World*, p. 49
15 Gleeson, p. 130; Bessborough, p. 7; p. 74
16 Foreman, p. 3; Bessborough, p. x
17 L.C.L., *Works*, Vol. 2, p. xi; Airlie, pp. xiv–xv; HARY-O, *Letters*, pp. 3–4; p. 9
18 Douglass, p. 19; H.A.L.S, D/Elb F 64
19 Bessborough, p. 56; L.C.L., *Letters*, p. 54
20 L.C.L., *Letters*, p. 9
21 Bessborough, p. 13; p. 60; p. 63
22 Ibid., p. 73
23 Foreman, pp. 276–7
24 Douglass, pp. 32–4
25 Lees-Milne, p. 6; Askwith, p. 24
26 Hayter, p. 38 *et seq.*
27 Miller, p. 42 *et seq.*; Douglass & March, p. 35 *et seq.*
28 Airlie, p. 51
29 Douglass, p. 37
30 Bessborough, p. 121

CHAPTER TWO:
MORTAL BRIDE
1 Mitchell, p. 60
2 Foreman, p. 385 & note
3 Airlie, p. 17; Douglass, p. 57
4 Cecil, p. 36
5 Airlie, p. 77
6 Mitchell, p. 60
7 Lees-Milne, p. 8 *et seq.*
8 L.C.L., *Works*, Vol. 2, pp. 103–4
9 Airlie, p. 65
10 Cecil, p. 97

11 Mitchell, p. 61; Panshanger MSS, D/Elb fol. 12
12 Airlie, p. xiv; Mitchell, p. 60
13 Douglass, p. 47; Bessborough, p. xii
14 Ziegler, p. 45; Foster, p. 244
15 Foster, p. 232
16 Ponsonby, pp. 130–31
17 Morgan, Vol. 1, p. 443
18 Ziegler, p. 48; L.C.L., *Letters*, pp. 20–21
19 Wilson, *Courtesan*, p. 46; L.C.L., *Letters*, pp. 38–9
20 L.C.L., *Letters*, p. 41; L.C.L., *Letters*, p. 22
21 Foreman, p. 391; HARY-O, *Letters*, p. 152
22 Mitchell, p. 90
23 L.C.L., *Letters*, p. 229
24 Fraser, *Perilous Question*, pp. 31–2
25 Hansard, 19 Nov. 1806
26 L.C.L., *Letters*, pp. 23–4
27 HARY-O, *Letters*, p. 211; Douglass, p. 77
28 Brown, p. 181
29 HARY-O, *Letters*, p. 229

CHAPTER THREE:
WHAT A WORLD
1 Ziegler, p. 46
2 Douglass, pp. 76–7; HARY-O, *Letters*, p. 257; L.C.L., *Letters*, p. 40
3 Lyttelton, p. 79
4 L.C.L., *Letters*, p. 51
5 HARY-O, *Letters*, pp. 235–6
6 Ibid., p. 223
7 Fraser, *Perilous Question*, p. 53
8 Bessborough, p. 155; Douglass, p. 63
9 Bessborough, p. 155
10 HARY-O, *Letters*, p. 133; p. 9
11 Lees-Milne, p. 13

12 HARY-O, *Letters*, p. 166
13 Bessborough, p. 199
14 Greville, p. 64; Douglass, p. 137
15 L.C.L., *Letters*, p. 57
16 Ibid., pp. 58–9
17 Ibid. p. 56; Douglass, p. 86
18 G.E.C., Holland, Vol. 4, p. 42, note e; Cecil, pp. 120–21
19 Foster, p. 416; Brown, p. 186
20 L.C.L., *Letters*, pp. 52–4
21 Fraser, *Caroline Norton*, pp. 73–4; L.C.L., *Letters*, p. 1
22 Hobhouse, Vol. 1, p. 194
23 Greville, Vol. 1, p. 99; H.A.L.S, D/Elb f. 32/3
24 L.C.L., *Letters*, p. 64
25 Douglass, pp. 96–7
26 L.C.L., *Letters*, pp. 54–5
27 Ibid., p. 74
28 Ibid., p. 56; Douglass, p. 97

CHAPTER FOUR:
THE THRILLING LYRE
1 L.C.L., *Letters*, p. 78
2 Cecil, pp. 125–6
3 MacCarthy, p. 146
4 Medwin, p. 7 *et seq.*
5 Foster, p. 376
6 See Byron, *Works*, *Childe Harold*
7 Douglass, pp. 82–3
8 Morgan, Vol. 2, pp. 200–201; p. 254
9 MacCarthy, pp. 145–6
10 Ponsonby, p. 133
11 Morgan, Vol. 2, p. 200
12 MacCarthy, p. 167
13 L.C.L., *Letters*, pp. 279–80
14 See Byron, *Works*, *Childe Harold*
15 Childers, pp. 81–95; Bessborough, pp. 226–7
16 Cecil, p. 123

17 Clarissa Eden, p. 80
18 Brown, p. 193
19 Airlie, p. 4 *et seq.*
20 MacCarthy, p. 180; Byron, *L. & J.*, Vol. 2, pp. 170–71
21 L.C.L., *Letters*, p. 81
22 Byron, *L. & J.*, Vol. 2, pp. 170–71
23 Marchand, p. 127
24 Byron, *L. & J.*, Vol. 2, p. 177 & note
25 Douglass, p. 114; Byron, *L. & J.*, Vol. 2, p. 177
26 L.C.L., *Letters*, pp. 83–4
27 Ibid., p. 82; p. 84
28 Cecil, p. 97
29 Airlie, p. 108
30 Seymour, p. 36; p. 33; Medwin, p. 32
31 Medwin, p. 32; Pakenham, *Soldier*, p. 113; Seymour, p. 24
32 Seymour, pp. 25–6
33 Foster, p. 362; Elwin, p. 109; Seymour, p. 32
34 Elwin, p. 104
35 Ibid., p. 113
36 Seymour, pp. 25–6

CHAPTER FIVE:
THAT MOMENT
1 Marchand, *Biography*, Vol. 1, p. 355 *et seq.*
2 L.C.L., *Letters*, p. 120
3 Douglass, p. 116 *et seq.*
4 Granville, Vol. 2, p. 448 *et seq.*
5 Douglass, p. 123
6 Byron, *L. & J.*, Vol. 2, p. 185
7 L.C.L., *Letters*, pp. 86–7
8 L.C.L., *Works*, Vol. 2, p. 103; Foreman, p. 385 note
9 See Small, *passim*
10 Ibid., p. 33
11 Stone, Annexe, Brown, pp. 248–9

12 Bessborough, p. 215; p. 222
13 Brown, p. 201
14 O'Byrne, pp. 149–50
15 Granville, Vol. 2, p. 460 *et seq.*
16 Ibid., p. 463
17 Ibid., p. 462
18 Lees-Milne, p. 22
19 Ibid., p. 23
20 Powell, p. 191
21 Byron, *L. & J.*, Vol. 2, p. 194; p. 226 note 1
22 Creevey Papers, p. 255; MacCarthy, p. 186
23 Creevey Papers, p. 255; Byron, *L. & J.*, Vol. 2, p. 258 note 2
24 Ibid., Vol. 2, p. 259
25 Granville, Vol. 2, p. 467 note 1
26 Douglass, p. 139

CHAPTER SIX:
YE DAGGER SCENE
1 Douglass, p. 144
2 Byron, *L. & J.*, Vol. 3, pp. 8–9
3 Ibid., p. 12
4 Byron, *L. & J.*, Vol. 2, p. 333
5 Marchand, pp. 141–2
6 Andrew Stauffer, cit. Douglass, p. 144 & p. 319 ref. 7
7 Marchand, p. 142
8 Bessborough, p. 239
9 Gleeson, p. 312 note
10 Bessborough, p. 232
11 Seymour, p. 44 *et seq.*
12 Ridley, p. 42
13 MacCarthy, p. 202
14 Douglass, p. 153
15 Birkenhead, p. 94; Cecil, p. 146
16 Wetherall-Dickson, *Madness*, p. 42 note 7
17 Douglass, p. 144
18 Ziegler, p. 55
19 Morgan, Vol. 1, pp. 441–2
20 Byron, *L. & J.*, Vol. 4, p. 19

21 See Bertie, *passim*; Phillips, *passim*
22 Nathan, *Fugitive Pieces*, p. 149 *et seq.*
23 Marchand, p. 92
24 Phillips, p. 39
25 Nathan & Byron, p. 3 *et seq.*

CHAPTER SEVEN:
ACTIVE IN PARIS
1 Seymour, p. 65
2 Medwin, p. 69 note 182
3 L.C.L., *Letters*, pp. 132–3
4 BL Add MSS 51560 fol. 199
5 Longford, p. 10
6 Bessborough, pp. 249–50
7 L.C.L., *Letters*, p. 132; Greville, p. 7
8 Ponsonby, p. 121; Foster, p. 405
9 Gleeson, p. 365
10 L.C.L., *Letters*, p. 134
11 Ibid., pp. 125–36
12 Ibid., p. 137
13 Longford, p. 19; p. 12
14 Askwith, p. 90
15 H.G., *Letters*, Vol. 1, pp. 64–5
16 Ibid., p. 74
17 Muir, p. 179
18 Longford, p. 35
19 BOD MSS Eng lett c.708 fol. 33
20 Mitchell, p. 74
21 Longford, p. 30
22 MacCarthy, p. 130; Douglass, p. 174
23 Mitchell, p. 74
24 Douglass, p. 187
25 BOD MSS Eng C 5753 fol. 128 r
26 BOD MSS Eng C 5753 fol. 128 v

CHAPTER EIGHT: PASSION
1 L.C.L., *Letters*, p. 129
2 Foster, *Duchesses*, pp. 430–31; MacCarthy, p. 263
3 L.C.L., *Letters*, p. 138
4 Ibid., pp. 141–2
5 Ibid., p. 145
6 Morgan, Vol. 2, p. 202
7 L.C.L., *Letters*, pp. 149–50
8 Douglass, p. 170
9 Ibid., p.184
10 Marchand, p. 228
11 See L.C.L., *Glenarvon*
12 Byron, *L. & J.*, Vol. 2, p. 242

CHAPTER NINE:
POOR CALANTHA!
1 Small, p. 152
2 Pakenham, *Edgeworth*, p. 202
3 Morgan, Vol. 2, pp. 201–2
4 Ibid., p. 203
5 Granville, Vol. 2, p. 542
6 Morgan, Vol. 2, p. 202
7 Cecil, p. 161; Paterson-Morgan, p. 49
8 Douglass, p. 189
9 Wellington MSS 20 July 1816; 26 July 1816; 7 October 1816
10 Wellington MSS 13 January 1817
11 Wellington Archives, info. received
12 Wellington MSS 18 November 1817
13 MacCarthy, p. 275; p. 278
14 Ibid., p. 302; Marchand, *Byron*, Vol. 2, p. 642
15 Marchand, *Byron*, Vol. 2, pp. 615–16
16 Byron, *L. & J.*, Vol. 2, p. 242 note 1
17 L.C.L., *Letters*, pp. 151–3
18 Byron, *L. & J.*, Vol. 6, p. 115; p. 248

19 Ibid., Vol. 7, p. 37 & note
20 L.C.L., *Letters*, p. 155
21 Ibid., p. 154
22 See Dickinson
23 Mitchell, p. 67; BL MS45550
    14 August 1825
24 Cecil, p. 161; Douglass, p. 181
25 H.G., *Letters*, Vol. 1, p. 90

CHAPTER TEN:
COME TO BROCKET HALL
1 Douglass, p. 275; Wilson, p.
    115; p. 168
2 Mitchell, p. 80 *et seq.*
3 See Howell-Thomas *passim.*
4 Ibid., p. 13
5 Vincent, p. 71
6 Mitchell, p. 110
7 L.C.L., *Letters*, p. 165
8 Vincent, p. 15
9 Ibid., p. 33
10 Blyth, p. 218
11 Vincent, p. 71
12 L.C.L., *Letters*, p. 166
13 Nathan, *Fugitive Pieces*, pp.
    151–2
14 Byron, *Works, Don Juan*
15 Byron, *L. & J.*, Vol. 6, p. 257
    & note 1; MacCarthy, p. 367
16 L.C.L., *Works*, Vol. 2, pp.
    143–9; Douglass, p. 220 *et seq.*
17 L.C.L., *Works*, Vol. 2, p. xxiii
18 Brown, p. 243
19 Airlie, *Palmerston*, Vol. 1, p. 43
20 Ibid., p. 41
21 Wilson, p. 83
22 Douglass, p. 224
23 Byron, *L. & J.*, Vol. 6, p. 169
    & note
24 *Godwin*, Vol. 2, p. 267
25 Douglass, p. 215
26 L.C.L., *Letters*, pp. 172–3
27 Byron, *L. & J.*, Vol. 6, p. 107
28 Gleeson, p. 355 *et seq.*

CHAPTER ELEVEN:
WRECK OF A LITTLE BOAT
1 H.A.L.S., Lytton MSS DE/K c.
    28 fol. 29
2 Sadleir, p. 58
3 Mitchell, *Bulwer*, p. 15
4 H.A.L.S., D/Elb F 62
5 *Godwin*, Vol. 2, pp. 267–8
6 L.C.L., *Letters*, p. 176;
    Godwin, Vol. 2, p. 285
7 *Godwin*, Vol. 2., p. 285 *et seq.*
8 Ibid., p. 285
9 L.C.L., *Works*, Vol. 2
10 Douglass, p. 231
11 L.C.L., *Works*, Vol. 2; Mitchell,
    p. 79; Cecil, p. 192
12 L.C.L., *Works*, Vol. 3
13 *Palmerston*, pp. 22–3; L.C.L.,
    Letters, p. 178
14 Wetherall-Dickson, *Authority*,
    p. 385; L.C.L., *Letters*, p. 178
15 Douglass, p. 251; L.C.L.,
    Works, Vol. 3, Intro p. vii
16 L.C.L., *Works*, Vol. 3, p. 44
17 Ibid., Vol. 2, p. 187
18 E. Melbourne, p. 273
19 *Palmerston*, p. 111
20 L.C.L., *Letters*, p. 205
21 Marchand, p. 171
22 L.C.L., *Letters*, p. 205;
    Douglass, p. 263; *Palmerston*,
    p. 135
23 Wellington MSS, Letter 184
24 Wellington MSS, Letter 307
25 Wellington MSS, Letter 308;
    309
26 L.C.L., *Letters*, pp. 202–3
27 Douglass, p. 267
28 Mitchell, p. 83
29 Wilson, *Courtesan*, p. 225
30 Ibid., p. 350; L.C.L., *Works*,
    Vol. 2, p. 192
31 L.C.L., *Works*, p. 188
32 Mitchell, p. 111

33 L.C.L., *Letters*, p. 212

CHAPTER TWELVE:
MELANCHOLY
1 West Sussex RO, MSS 182
2 Cecil, p. 36
3 Mitchell, p. 26
4 L.C.L., *Letters*, p. 209; Nathan, *Fugitive Pieces*, p. 190
5 BL MSS 4 5550
6 L.C.L., *Letters*, p. 212; Airlie, *Palmerston*, Vol. 1, p. 122
7 L.C.L., *Works*, Vol. 2, p. 103
8 Nathan, *Fugitive Pieces*, p. 183
9 Wellington MSS Letter 309 27 August 1824
10 L.C.L., *Letters*, p. 215
11 Douglass, p. 274
12 Mulvey-Roberts, Vol. 3, pp. 12–15
13 *Godwin*, p. 303
14 Ibid.
15 Howell-Thomas, p. 50
16 Ibid., p. 46; West Sussex RO, MSS 161

17 MacCarthy, p. 540; Douglas, pp. 231–2
18 L.C.L., *Letters*, p. 206
19 L.C.L., *Letters*, p. 216
20 Douglass, p. 283
21 Bessborough, p. 292
22 Ziegler, p. 105

EPILOGUE:
REMEMBER THEE!
1 QVJ, 3 March 1838
2 H.G., *Letters*, Vol. 2, p. 9
3 QVJ, 1 January 1838
4 Howell-Thomas, p. 136
5 Phillips, p. 107 *et seq.*
6 *Godwin*, p. 303; L.C.L., *Letters*, p. 56
7 Byron, *L. & J.*, Vol. 2, p. 170
8 Morgan, Vol. 2, pp. 253–4
9 Milton, *Paradise Lost*, Book One

SOURCES

Note:
Editions are hardback, published in London, unless otherwise stated.

L.C.L. stands for Lady Caroline Lamb, as in L.C.L., *Letters*.

Hansard dates refer to on-line entry. See Hansard below.

A

[Airlie] Airlie, Mabell Countess of, *In Whig Society, 1775–1818, compiled from the hitherto unpublished correspondence of Elizabeth Viscountess Melbourne and Emily Countess Cowper, afterwards Viscountess Palmerston*, 1921

Airlie, Mabell Countess of, *Lady Palmerston and her Times*, 2 vols, 1922

Askwith, Betty, *Piety and Wit. A Biography of Harriet Countess Granville, 1785–1862*, 1982

B

Bertie, Charles H., *Isaac Nathan: Australia's First Composer: A Lecture Delivered at the Conservatorium of Music, Sydney*, with a Foreword by Henri Verbrugghen, 1972

Bessborough, The Earl of, ed. in collaboration with A. Aspinall, PhD, *Lady Bessborough and her Family Circle*, 1940

Birkenhead, Sheila, *Peace in Piccadilly: The Story of Albany*, 1958

[BL] British Library, London, MSS

Blyth, Henry, *Caro – The Fatal Passion: The Life of Lady Caroline Lamb*, New York, 1972

[BOD] Bodleian Library, University of Oxford, MSS

Brown, Colin, *Lady M: The Life and Lovers of Elizabeth Lamb, Viscountess Melbourne 1751–1818*, 2018

[Byron, *L. & J.*] *Byron's Letters and Journals*, ed. Leslie A. Marchand, and Index, 12 vols, 1973–82

[Byron, *Works*] *Lord Byron: The Major Works*, ed. with Introduction and notes Jerome J. McGann, revised edn, pbk, Oxford, 2000

C

Cecil, Lord David, *The Young Melbourne and Lord M*, pbk, 2001

Chambers, Paul, *Bedlam: London's Hospital for the Mad*, pbk, 2019

Childers, William, 'Byron's "Waltz": The Germans and their Georges', *Keats-Shelley Journal*, 18, 1969

Clarissa Eden – A Memoir: From Churchill to Eden, ed. Cate Haste, 2007

Clarke, Tim, *The Countess: The Scandalous Life of Frances Villiers, Countess of Jersey, 1753–1821*, pbk, 2019

Creevey Papers, ed. Sir Herbert Maxwell, Vol. 1, 1905

D

Devonshire MSS, Devonshire Collection Archives and Library, Chatsworth, Bakewell, Derbyshire

Dickinson, Hilary, 'Accounting for Augustus Lamb: Theoretical and Methodological Issues in Biography and Historical Sociology', *Sociology*, 27(1), February 1993

[Douglass] Douglass, Paul, *Lady Caroline Lamb: A Biography*, 2004

Douglass, Paul & March, Rosemary, 'That "Vital Spark of Genius"', *Pacific Coast Philology*, 41, 2006

E

Elwin, Malcolm, *Lord Byron's Wife*, 1962

Esher, Viscount (ed.), *The Girlhood of Queen Victoria: A Selection from Her Majesty's Diaries between the Years 1832 and 1840*, 2 vols, 1912

F

Foreman, Amanda, *Georgiana Duchess of Devonshire*, 1998

Foster, Vere (ed.), *The Two Duchesses: Georgiana, Duchess of Devonshire, Elizabeth, Duchess of Devonshire. Family Correspondence . . .*, 1898

Fraser, Antonia, *The Case of the Married Woman: Caroline Norton – A 19th-Century Heroine Who Wanted Justice for Women*, 2021

Fraser, Antonia, *Perilous Question: The Drama of the Great Reform Bill 1832*, pbk, 2014

G

[G.E.C.] G.E. Cockayne, *The Complete Peerage of England, Scotland, Ireland, Great Britain and the United Kingdom*, 13 vols, reprint 1982

Gleeson, Janet, *Privilege and Scandal: The Remarkable Life of Harriet Spencer, Sister of Georgiana*, pbk, New York, 2007

[*Godwin*] Kegan Paul, C., *William Godwin: Friends and Contemporaries*, 2 vols, 1876

Grant, Colin, *A Smell of Burning: A Memoir of Epilepsy*, pbk, 2016

[Granville] Granville Leveson-Gower, Lord (1st Earl Granville), *Private Correspondence 1781 to 1821*, 2 vols, 1916

The Greville Memoirs 1814–1860, ed. Lytton Strachey & Roger Fulford, Vol. 1, January 1814 to July 1830, 193

H

[H.A.L.S.] Hertfordshire Archives, County Hall, Herts.

[Hansard] http://hansard.millbanksystems.com/commons

[HARY-O, *Letters*] HARY-O: The Letters of Lady Harriet Cavendish 1796–1809, ed. by her grandson, Sir George Leveson-Gower, KBE, and his daughter Iris Palmer, 1940

Hayter, Alethea, '"The Laudanum Bottle Loomed Large":

Opium in the English Literary World in the Nineteenth Century', *Ariel*, 2 (4), 1980

[H.G., *Letters*] *Letters of Harriet Countess Granville 1810–1845*, ed. her son, the Hon. F. Leveson-Gower, 2 vols, 1894

[Hist. Parlt.] *The History of Parliament: The House of Commons*, ed. D.R. Fisher, 7 vols, 2009

[Hobhouse] Lord Broughton (John Cam Hobhouse), *Recollections of a Long Life*, ed. Lady Dorchester, 2 vols, 1910–11

Howell-Thomas, Dorothy, *Lord Melbourne's Susan*, Foreword by Robert Gittings, Surrey, 1978

I J K

Kelly, Linda, *Richard Brinsley Sheridan: A Life*, 1997

Knox, Clement, *Strange Antics: A History of Seduction*, 2020

L

Langley Moore, Doris, *The Late Lord Byron: Posthumous Dramas*, 1961

[L.C.L.] Lady Caroline Lamb, *Glenarvon*, Introduction by Frances Wilson, pbk, 1995

[L.C.L., *Letters*] *The Whole Disgraceful Truth: Selected Letters of Lady Caroline Lamb*, ed. Paul Douglass, 2006

[L.C.L., *Works*] *The Works of Lady Caroline Lamb*, ed. Leigh Wetherall Dickson & Paul Douglass, 3 vols, 2009

Lees-Milne, James, *The Bachelor Duke: A Life of William Spencer Cavendish, 6th Duke of Devonshire 1790–1858*, 1991

Longford, Elizabeth, *Wellington: Pillar of State*, 1972

[Lyttelton] *Correspondence of Sarah Spencer, Lady Lyttelton, 1787–1870*, ed. The Hon. Mrs Hugh Wyndham, 1912

[Lytton] Lytton, The Earl of, *The Life of Edward Bulwer, 1st Lord Lytton. By his Grandson*, 2 vols, 1913

[*Life of Lytton*] *The Life, Letters and Literary Remains of Edward Bulwer, Lord Lytton. By his son*, 2 vols, 1883

Rosina Bulwer Lytton: A Blighted Life, with a new Introduction by Marie Mulvey-Roberts, Bristol, 1994

M

MacCarthy, Fiona, *Byron: Life and Legend*, pbk, 2014

Marchand, Leslie A., *Byron: A Biography*, 3 vols, 1959

[Marchand] Marchand, Leslie A., *Byron: A Portrait*, pbk, 1993

Marshall, Dorothy, *Lord Melbourne*, Introduction by A.J.P. Taylor, 1975

Medwin's Conversations of Lord Byron. Revised with a new Preface by the Author for a New Edition . . ., ed. Ernest J. Lovell Jr, Princeton, N.J., pbk, 1966

[Melbourne, E.] Melbourne, Elizabeth Milbanke Lamb, Viscountess, *Byron's 'Corbeau Blanc': The Life and Letters of Lady Melbourne*, ed. Jonathan David Gross, Houston, Tex., 1997

Miller, Lucasta, *L.E.L.: The Lost Life and Scandalous Death of Letitia Elizabeth Landon, the celebrated 'Female Byron'*, New York, 2019

[Mitchell] Mitchell, Leslie, *Lord Melbourne 1779–1848*, Oxford, 1997

Mitchell, Leslie, *Bulwer Lytton: The Rise and Fall of a Victorian Man of Letters*, 2003

Mitchell, Leslie, *Holland House*, 1980

Mitchell, Leslie, *The Whig World 1760–1837*, pbk, 2007

[Morgan] *Lady Morgan's Memoirs: Autobiography, Diaries and Correspondence*, ed. W. Hepworth Dixon, 2 vols, 1862

Muir, Rory, *Wellington: Waterloo and the Fortunes of Peace*, 2015

Mulvey-Roberts, Marie (ed.), *The Collected Letters of Rosina Bulwer-Lytton*, Vol. 3, with the assistance of Steve Carpenter, 2008

N

Nathan, Isaac, *Fugitive Pieces and Reminiscences of Lord Byron: containing an entirely new edition of the Hebrew Melodies . . . Also some Original Poetry and Recollections of Lady Caroline Lamb*, 1829, reprint

[Nathan & Byron] *A Selection of Hebrew Melodies, Ancient and Modern, by Isaac Nathan and Lord Byron*, ed. with

Introduction by Frederick Burwick and Paul Douglass, 1988

O

O'Byrne, Robert, *Left Without a Handkerchief*, 2022

P

Pakenham, Eliza, *Soldier, Sailor: An Intimate Portrait of an Irish Family*, 2007

Pakenham, Valerie, selected & ed., *Maria Edgeworth's Letters from Ireland*, Dublin, 2018

Letters of Lady Palmerston, selected & ed. from the originals at Broadlands and elsewhere, Tresham Lever, 1957

Panshanger MSS, Hertfordshire Archives, County Hall, Herts.

Paterson-Morgan, Emily, 'She Does Paint Most Delightfully: Lady Caroline Lamb's Artistic Accomplishments', *The Byron Journal*, 50(1), 2022

Phillips, Olga Somech, *Isaac Nathan: Friend of Byron*, 1940

Ponsonby, Major-General Sir John, KCB, *The Ponsonby Family*, 1920

Porter, Roy, *A Social History of Madness: Stories of the Women*, 1987

Powell, Anthony, *The Valley of Bones*, pbk, 2019

Q

[QVJ] Queen Victoria's Journals, http://www/.queenvictorias journals

R

Ridley, Jasper, *Lord Palmerston*, 1970

S

Sadleir, Michael, *Bulwer: A Panorama, Edward and Rosina, 1803–1836*, 1931

[Seymour] Seymour, Miranda, *In Byron's Wake: The Turbulent Lives of Lord Byron's Wife and Daughter: Annabella Milbanke and Ada Lovelace*, 2018

Seymour, Miranda, *Mary Shelley*, pbk, 2018

Shaw, Karl, *Mad, Bad and Dangerous to Know*, pbk, 2017

Small, Helen, *Love's Madness: Medicine, the Novel and Female Insanity, 1800–1865*, pbk reprint, Oxford, 2007

Spencer, Charles, *The Spencer Family*, 1999

Stone, Dr James, see Brown, *Lady M.*, Annexe, pp. 248–9

Stourton, James, *Great Houses of London*, 2012

T

Thompson, William and Wheeler, Anne, *Appeal of One Half of the Human Race, Women, Against the Pretensions of the Other Half, Men*, with a new Introduction by the Rt Hon. Richard Foot and Marie Mulvey-Roberts, Bristol, 1994

U

Usher, Howard, *Fatal Females: Elizabeth Lady Melbourne and Emily Lady Palmerston: A Mother and Daughter Partnership*, The Melbourne Trust, 1990

V

Vincent, E.R., *Ugo Foscolo: An Italian in Regency England*, pbk, New York, 1953

W

Wellington Archives, Stratfield Saye, Hants.

West Sussex Record Office, County Hall, Chichester

Wetherall-Dickson, Leigh, 'Authority and Legitimacy: The Cultural Context of Lady Caroline Lamb's Novels', *Women's Writing*, 13(3), October 2006

Wetherall-Dickson, Leigh, 'The Construction of a Reputation of Madness: The Case Study of Lady Caroline Lamb', *Working with English*, 2, 2005–8

Wetherall-Dickson, Leigh, 'A Written Warning: Lady Caroline Lamb, Noblesse Oblige and the works of John Ford', in *Shakespeare and the Culture of Romanticism*, ed. Joseph M. Ortiz, 2013, pp. 245–66

Wilson, Frances (ed.), *Byromania: Portraits of the Artist in Nineteenth- and Twentieth-Century Culture*, New York, 1999

Wilson, Frances, *The Courtesan's Revenge: Harriette Wilson, the Woman who Blackmailed the King*, 2003

[Wilson, *Memoirs*] *The Memoirs of Harriette Wilson: English Classics*, ed. Eveleigh Nash, 2 vols, reprint, 2016

X Y Z

Zanou, Konstantina, 'Ugo Foscolo: A Life of Stammering in Exile', in *Transnational Patriotism in the Mediterranean 1800–1852: Stammering the Nation*, Oxford, 2018

Ziegler, Philip, *Melbourne: A Biography of William Lamb, 2nd Viscount Melbourne*, 2013

ACKNOWLEDGEMENTS

In researching and writing this book I have benefited from the advice and help of many people to whom I am most grateful. I wish to thank:

The Marquess and Marchioness of Salisbury for hospitality at Hatfield House and a visit to St Etheldreda's Church; David Mott, Senior Building Manager, for an instructive tour of the Scotland Office at Dover House (formerly Melbourne House) and Alex Chisholm for arranging it; Lord Ralph Kerr and Mrs Gill Weston for information about Melbourne Hall, Derbyshire; John and Virginia Murray for an illuminating visit to John Murray Publishers, 50 Albemarle Street.

My visit to Brocket Hall, arranged by Emma Irving, was a highlight of my self-styled Optical Research, beginning with the benevolence of Dame Penelope Wilton in acting as my chauffeur; then Juliet Appleby was a most helpful guide. I wish to thank Damon de Laszlo for welcoming me to Byron's set at Albany, and Ariane Bankes for arranging it.

A considerable part of my research took place during the difficult period of lockdown, which makes me especially grateful to archivists for their helpful responses. I wish to thank Lord Bessborough for information and Abigail Hartley, Searchroom Archivist, West Sussex Record Office; Richard Ovenden, Bodley's Librarian, and Lisa Dotsauer, Senior Library Assistant, Bodleian Library; Jamie Andrews and Catherine Angerson, British Library; Fran Baker, Archivist and Librarian, Chatsworth; Lynn Burton, Archive Library Assistant, Heritage Services, Hertford Archives and Local Studies; Kirsty McHugh, National Library of Scotland;

Jane Branfield, Archivist, Stratfield Saye House; Bernardette Archer, National Art Library, and Jack Glover Gunn, Imaging Executive, Victoria & Albert Museum; Victoria Webb, Librarian, Wellcome Collection.

I am most grateful to the Duke of Devonshire for permission to use the portrait of Lady Caroline Lamb on the cover of the book which was commissioned by the 6th Duke and still hangs at Chatsworth; and to the Duke of Wellington for permission to use the copy of *Glenarvon* with Lady Caroline Lamb's personal dedication to his great ancestor as an illustration.

Then there are the many books, the silent supports, all acknowledged with gratitude. Pre-eminent among them is the most recent scholarly study of the subject, Professor Paul Douglass's outstanding biography, *Lady Caroline Lamb*, 2004, and the invaluable follow-up, *The Whole Disgraceful Truth: Selected Letters of Lady Caroline Lamb*, 2006. Sources gives the full list of books consulted.

I also wish to thank Professor Leslie Mitchell, for critical help once again; Dr Ambrogio Caiani for help over Ugo Foscolo; Eliza Chisholm; Rupert Gavin; Rana Kabbani; Marie Mulvey-Roberts; Michael Neill; Robert O'Byrne for illumination about Irish country houses; Valerie Pakenham; Dr Emily Paterson-Morgan, Director, *The Byron Society*; Miranda Seymour; Anne Somerset for helpful references to Queen Victoria's Journals; Natalie Speir; Charles Spencer; Hugo Vickers, as ever an impeccable source on royal matters; and Dr Leigh Wetherall-Dickson.

Early readers were Alan Samson, my friend and former publisher, Victoria Gray, and Mike Shaw: I am grateful for their encouragement. Jonathan Lloyd has as ever been a strong support, always answering when I call my agent.

Antonia Fraser

LIST OF ILLUSTRATIONS

18 Lord Byron's chambers, Albany (Courtesy of Damon de Laszlo)

19 Annabella Milbanke (Picture Art Collection/Alamy Stock Photo)

20 Duke of Wellington (By permission of The Wellington College)

21 Brocket Hall, Essex (Antiqua Print Gallery/Alamy Stock Photo)

22 John Murray (Zuri Swimmer/Alamy Stock Photo)

23 *Glenarvon* (Stratfield Saye Preservation Trust)

24 Michael Bruce (National Portrait Gallery, London)

25 Poem by Lady Caroline Lamb (Bodleian Library Archives)

26 Ugo Foscolo (Art Collection 2/Alamy Stock Photo)

27 Isaac Nathan (History Collection/Alamy Stock Photo)

28 Bulwer Lytton (Alamy Stock Photo)

29 Lady Caroline with her son Augustus (John Murray Archive/National Library of Scotland)

30 Letter to Caroline from Augustus (Courtesy of Myles Ponsonby, 12th Early of Bessborough)

31 St Etheldreda's Church, Hatfield (Peter Moulton/Alamy Stock Photo)

INDEX

Viscount *see* Leveson-Gower, Lord
Granville
Granville, Harriet Leveson-Gower,
Viscountess *see* Cavendish, Lady
Harriet ('Harryo')
Grenville, William Grenville, 1st
Baron, 30
Greville, Charles, 41, 45, 101
Grey, Charles Grey, 2nd Earl, 5, 14,
151
Guiccoli, Teresa, 127, 144, 165

Hamilton, Caroline (*née* Pakenham),
106–7
Hardwicke, Philip Yorke, 3rd Earl of,
105
Harley, Lady Charlotte, 79, 83, 140
Harrow School, 13, 55, 86
Hartington, William Cavendish,
Marquess of ('Hart'; *later* 6th
Duke of Devonshire): birth, 4, 23;
childhood, youth and upbringing,
16; relations with and views
on Caroline, 4, 16, 22–3, 37,
41–2; and Caroline's marriage to
William Lamb, 22–3; and father's
relationship with Elizabeth Foster,
40; early adulthood, 41–2, 60, 71;
inheritance of dukedom, 77–8;
restoration of Lismore Castle, 78;
commissions portrait of Caroline,
89–90; relationship with Princess
Charlotte, 103; in Paris, 103, 104;
and death of Caroline's mother,
147; and support for William
Godwin, 151; and Caroline's legal
Separation, 159
Hatfield, Hertfordshire, St
Etheldreda's Church, 32, 143, 172
Hatfield House, Hertfordshire, 85,
135, 168
Heathcote, Katherine, Lady, 88
Hobhouse, John (*later* 1st Baron
Broughton), 45, 69–70, 92, 120–1,
126–7, 144–5, 157
Holland, Elizabeth Fox, Lady (*née*
Vassall), 17, 32, 38–9, 42, 43, 46–7,
48, 58, 62, 100–1, 120, 123
Holland, Henry (architect), 27, 28

Holland, Henry Fox, 1st Baron, 38
Holland, Henry Vassall-Fox, 3rd
Baron, 17, 38–9, 43, 58, 122,
137–8
Holland House set, 38–9, 58
Homer, *The Iliad*, 138, 139
Hope, Thomas, 159
Hoppner, John, 20
Hornam, Horace, 61
horse-riding, 12, 19, 34, 48, 75, 90,
133
Howard, George (*later* 7th Earl of
Carlisle), 19
Hucknall Torkard, Nottinghamshire,
157
Hume, David, 29, 32, 59

illegitimacy, 4, 15–16, 38, 146
Ireland, 8, 75–9, 116, 162–3, 164–5
Isle of Wight, 36–7

Jersey, Frances Villiers, Countess of,
87
Jersey, George Villiers, 5th Earl of,
87
Jersey, Sarah Villiers, Countess of,
87–8, 106, 123
Jews, 93
Josephine, Empress of the French, 107

Kauffman, Angelica, 9
Kinnaird, Douglas, 94, 127
Knebworth, Hertfordshire, 148
Knight, Richard Payne, *The Progress
of Civil Society*, 5

La Rochefoucauld, François de, 64
Lamb, Augustus (Caroline's son):
appearance and character, 85, 100,
129; birth, 33; christening, 33;
early childhood and education,
33–4, 36–7, 46, 47, 48, 78, 85–6,
90, 100–1, 118–19, 128–9, 133;
ill-health and learning difficulties,
36–7, 72, 85–6, 128–9, 134, 162–3;
later childhood and youth, 135,
146–7, 151; early adulthood, 162–3,
168–9, 173; and Caroline's death,
171; death and burial, 172, 174